LIVING
MAGICALLY

A New Vision of Reality

GILL EDWARDS

LIVING
MAGICALLY

A New Vision of Reality

piatkus

To our unseen friends
– with love and gratitude

PIATKUS

First published in Great Britain in 1991 by Piatkus Books
This paperback edition published in 2009 by Piatkus
Reprinted 2009

A CIP catalogue record for this book
is available from the British Library

ISBN 978-0-7499-3998-4

Printed and bound in the UK by
CPI Mackays, Chatham, ME5 8TD

Papers used by Piatkus are natural, renewable and recyclable
products sourced from well-managed forests and certified
in accordance with the rules of the Forest Stewardship Council.

Mixed Sources
Product group from well-managed
forests and other controlled sources
www.fsc.org Cert no. SGS-COC-004081
© 1996 Forest Stewardship Council

FSC

Piatkus
An imprint of
Little, Brown Book Group
100 Victoria Embankment
London EC4Y 0DY

An Hachette UK Company
www.hachette.co.uk

www.piatkus.co.uk

Contents

Do not accept this little, fenced-off aspect as yourself. The sun and ocean are as nothing beside what you are. The sunbeam sparkles only in the sunlight, and the ripple dances as it rests upon the ocean. Yet in neither sun nor ocean is the power that rests in you.

(A Course in Miracles)

Acknowledgments

Firstly, my thanks are due to Gill Bailey and Judy Piatkus for their courage and vision in accepting this book for publication — and to Beth Wood for her helpful comments and editing.

My thanks, too, to those who shared my metaphysical journey while I was writing the book — in particular to my precious friend Trina, and my brother Brian; my love for them spans this and many other lifetimes. Also to David C., for our warm and stimulating discussions, to Maritza for her sharing and Guy Dauncey for his excellent and timely advice. And my love and thanks to my parents for their endless love and support, for proof-reading the original manuscript with such care, and for listening to my 'crazy' ideas; I chose them well!

Deepest thanks to my hundreds of clients, many of whom have a permanent place in my heart, who have been such wonderful teachers and 'mirrors' over the years. I can only hope that I have given as much as I have received. (Note: All the case histories in Part Two are based upon one or more real people, but personal details have been changed to protect confidentiality.)

Finally, my deep love and gratitude to Lazaris for 'waking me up', and sharing his extraordinary teachings with our world, to Seth for showing me a metaphysical path, to Bartholomew for his wisdom and insight, to Orin and DaBen for my joyful and ever-expanding journeys with them and, of course, to my own guides. Without our unseen friends, this book would not have been written.

I gratefully acknowledge the following permissions granted:

NPN Publishing Inc — the copyright holder of all Lazaris materials — and Concept: Synergy, Palm Beach, Florida for permission to quote from the Lazaris material:*Lazaris Interviews, Book I*, 1988; *Lazaris Interviews, Book II*, 1988; *The Sacred Journey: You and Your Higher Self*, 1987; *Harnessing the Power of Your Destiny; Reality Creation: The Basics; Discovering the Adult; The Secrets of Manifesting What You Want; Programming What You Want; The Mystery and Magic of Co-Creation*. All rights reserved. H J Kramer, Tiburon, California for permission to quote from the following Orin books by Sanaya Roman: *Living with Joy*, 1986; *Personal Power Through Awareness*, 1986; *Spiritual Growth: Being Your Higher Self*, 1989; and *Creating Money*, 1988 (written with Duane Packer and DaBen). All rights reserved. Simon and Schuster, London for permission to quote from the following Seth books by Jane Roberts: *The Individual and The Nature of Mass Events*, 1982; *The Seth Material*, 1987; *The Nature of Personal Reality*, 1987; *The Nature of the Psyche*, 1987. All rights reserved. Foundation for Inner Peace, Tiburon, California, 1975 for permission to quote from *A Course in Miracles* (Arkana, 1985). All rights reserved. Choosing Light Inc, 1989 for extraction from *Bridge of Light* by LaUna Huffines, published by Bantam Books. All rights reserved. High Mesa Press, Taos, New, Mexico for permission to quote from the following Bartholomew books: *I Came As A Brother*, 1986; *From The Heart of A Gentle Brother*, 1987; *Reflections of An Elder Brother*, 1989. All rights reserved.

Introduction

I was reading in my garden on a warm, sunny afternoon in late September when my life changed. In a timeless moment, the trees, flowers, grass, houses, sky were transformed into a whirling, swirling mass — and, scooped up in the vortex, I blended seamlessly and rapturously with them. Somehow I had passed into a looking glass world, and 'reality' now appeared rather strange and comical. Everything was different. It was exhilarating, scary, thrilling beyond words. I felt intoxicated with a sense of adventure. Suddenly, I knew that *anything* was possible, that life was just a wondrous game — and that by reaching for our Dreams, by trusting, by having vision, that life could become truly magical ...

Shortly after graduating in psychology, in the late 1970s, I came across an extraordinary book by Jane Roberts, Seth Speaks, which challenged all my common-sense assumptions about the world. Seth describes himself as 'an energy personality essence no longer focussed in physical reality' — a conscious, disembodied being who uses the body of a living person (the channel) in order to communicate with us verbally. I had read avidly about mysticism and the paranormal since my early teens, and meditated daily — yet the idea of channelling left me deeply sceptical. I was open-minded about whether mediums might hear messages from discarnate beings, or even receive 'automatic writing'; but the notion of a higher consciousness speaking *directly* to us — well, it did seem a lot to swallow! They would be telling me God used the telephone next!

Yet Seth held a stunning perspective on life which deeply reverberated with my inner knowing. Reading Seth felt like coming Home. He spoke of physical reality as an illusion that we create, how our thoughts and beliefs magnetically attract events which 'mirror' our inner world, how we might expand our consciousness into countless other dimensions of reality. What's more, from what I knew about the new physics, what Seth said might 'make sense' in modern scientific terms.

The Seth books tackled many of life's great mysteries. Why are we here? What is the nature of reality? Is the future predestined? Why are some people 'lucky' while others suffer one trauma after another? If Seth was correct, then our orthodox ways of seeing the world — whether scientific or religious — were bogus and limiting, and by 'waking up' to our true nature, we could transform our lives.

After training as a clinical psychologist, I worked in the National Health Service for nearly a decade. Throughout this time, I zig-zagged between personal growth/therapy (which explores our individuality), sociopolitical approaches (which emphasise our connectedness) and spiritual paths such as metaphysics and Buddhism. It seemed clear to me that psychology and spirituality should not be split in this way that *together* they might help us to fully embody our spirit, to fulfil our potential, to reclaim our wholeness.

I knew that psychology would forever be limited without an awareness of the spiritual, the metaphysical — that a psychology without a soul projected a mere fleeting shadow of what we may be. On the other hand, I felt wary of spiritual paths which tried to bypass our humanity — which ignored the 'shadow side' of the self, encouraged us to suppress emotions and desires, or treated the body as an encumbrance to the spirit. Surely personality and soul, dark and light, matter and spirit — our feet of clay as well as our hearts of gold — were to be embraced as different aspects of our wholeness?

For twelve years, as I slowly integrated psychology and spirituality, I *believed* in metaphysics, and used it in my therapeutic work — but I was not ready to *know* it, *live* it, *embody* it. Then, one sunny afternoon, I was reading a book by 'Lazaris' when I shifted irreversibly into a metaphysical vision of reality. I suddenly *experienced* what, until then, had been mostly intellectual. In that moment, my twenty-year search within personal growth, psychology, the paranormal, beyond-the-quantum physics, mysticism and spiritual growth became a dancing, dazzling, synergistic whole, pulsating with life and potential. Since then, I have devoted myself full-time to teaching and practising metaphysics — and my inner and outer world have changed beyond recognition.

I scoured bookshops in Britain, Canada and the USA in a vain search for a book like *Living Magically* — a book which combines the teachings of mystics, scientists and channelled sources with a practical, down-to-earth, self-help format. Having seen metaphysics change people's lives dramatically — sometimes within hours — I felt passionately that these ideas should now reach a wider audience. This book is the result.

Living Magically is a psychospiritual approach to everyday life. It bridges the gap between psychology and spiritual practice, and reconciles the mystical and magical with our daily lives. It offers a startling vision of reality — a vision which turns our 'common sense' upside-down.

In Part One, I explore the new vision of reality which is emerging from the cutting edge of science, and the remarkable phenomenon of channelling. Then I summarise what channelled sources reveal about how we create our own reality, the nature of our lives, and the coming of a 'New Age'.

In Part Two, I combine the wisdom and insight of channelled sources with my own experience as a psycho-therapist and spiritual-seeker, showing how theory can be put into practice. Thus, Part Two offers a step-by-step guide to *applying* metaphysics in your everyday life, in *how* to 'live magically': a sketch-map for your own journey. It reveals how to manifest your Dreams, personally and globally; and how to grow through joy rather than struggle. It shows how to break through your old fears, blockages and limitations, and release the past. It helps you to 'listen to the whispers' from your Higher Self and to discover your life's purpose.

In sharing this new vision of reality, I constantly delight in helping others to 'remember' who they really are, to rediscover their inner wisdom and power, to trust in their own unique path — and to awaken to the magic and wonder of this incredible journey that we call life.

With love and blessings,
Gill Edwards
London, 1991

PART ONE
A New Vision of Reality

1
A Trick of the Light?

*Our ordinary mind always tries to persuade us
that we are nothing but acorns and that our
greatest happiness will be to become bigger,
fatter, shinier acorns; but that it is of interest only
to pigs. Our faith gives us knowledge of something much better: that we can become oak trees.*

(E. F. Schumacher)[1]

Where did the magic go? Do you remember those sun-
drenched days of childhood when playing in a woodland
stream or chasing friends across a lawn filled you with joy
and delight? Perhaps you believed in angels and fairies, or
wishing upon a star, in those far-off days – and the world
seemed full of moondust and miracles.

Somewhere along the way, the magic gets lost. Our
ability to be 'happy for no reason', to gasp in awe and
wonder, to dream the impossible dream and glimpse the
invisible realms is slowly buried beneath a mound of daily
demands and routines, rationality and cynicism. Life
begins to seem, at best, humdrum and ordinary, or at
worst, full of struggle and anxiety – and we simply focus
on getting through the days. Yet deep down, I believe we
have a nagging feeling that life isn't *meant* to be this way,
that there is 'more to life than this' – that a more joyous
and magical existence lies just beyond our reach.

The trouble is, we have been brainwashed. For the past
three hundred years scientists have persuaded us to believe
in a clockwork, mechanical universe in which life is a
random accident which 'happened' to emerge from the
primordial broth — an accident of astronomical unlikli-
hood, perhaps, but an accident nevertheless. (After all, they
haven't seen God down their microscopes, have they?)

Science has given birth to a nightmarish existence in which we are isolated cogs in a mundane world-machine, leading brief, meaningless lives while battling against the brutal forces of nature. Whatever does not fit this materialist world view — the mind, consciousness, experience, feelings, thoughts, intuition, love, wisdom, faith, God, spirituality, inspiration, creativity, myth, religion, art, ethics, psychic experiences, personal growth — has been declared irrelevant or even nonsensical, and has therefore been devalued. No wonder we live in an age of existential anxiety and despair! We have been deprived of our very humanity, our very souls.

Many believe that this mundane world view is based upon what is objectively true, what has been discovered, what is real. Yet science does not represent Truth any more than Grimm's fairy tales do. It is merely a form of storytelling, a poetic metaphor, a way-of-seeing. It is the current orthodoxy, the dogma of our culture, which dictates how we should view the world. Science cannot disprove that life has meaning and significance, since it is not designed even to *ask* such questions — yet it has still profoundly influenced how we think and feel about our lives.

We have created
solid walls
solid things
solid boundaries
solid lives
We think it of value if it matters
Matter is where we put our trust
not motion
or the spirit of life.

(Miller Mair)[2]

Curiously enough, religious dogma has also promoted the mundane world view. Both science and religion have portrayed humanity as the helpless pawns of forces beyond our control. While science sees our lives determined by laws of nature, or the whims of so-called 'chance' and 'coincidence', religion has pointed towards the (often cruel) dictates of God, fate or past karma. Either way, we are powerless.

Likewise, both science and religion have viewed the world as purely physical. While science simply pooh-poohs the non-physical and non-rational, religion often contrasts the mundaneness and suffering of life with the divinity and delight of 'heaven', viewing earthly life — with God as our absentee landlord — as something to be endured, until we ascend to the dubious pleasure of playing the harp for eternity, or vanish into the personal oblivion of Nirvana.

THE QUANTUM LEAP

However, our vision of reality is now undergoing a transformation so profound, so shattering, that it has been compared to the evolutionary leap which produced life on earth. Collectively, we are taking a quantum leap in consciousness — a leap towards rediscovering our connectedness with others; a leap towards inner wisdom and power; a leap towards awareness of other dimensions of reality; and a leap towards a breathtaking new perspective on our everyday lives. The implications for humanity as a whole are truly astonishing. As Henry Miller[3], puts it, 'We live at the edge of the miraculous.' A vision of a 'New Age' is indeed beginning to dawn.

Fritjof Capra, in his brilliant tour de force *The Turning Point*, shows that we are moving inexorably towards a new world view, and that the global crisis stems from clinging to our old model. The crisis, he notes, is one of perception.

Marilyn Ferguson, in *The Aquarian Conspiracy*, writes of the growing number of individuals, from all walks of life, who are awakening to a transcendent level of consciousness. A new vision is blossoming, she says, which promotes the idea 'that we are not victims, not pawns, not limited by conditions or conditioning. Heirs to evolutionary riches, we are capable of imagination, invention, and experiences we have only glimpsed.'[4]

Similarly, Peter Russell suggests in *The Awakening Earth* that we are on the threshold of an evolutionary leap, the extraordinary pace of which is likely to take us all by surprise. 'And the changes leading to this leap are taking place right before our eyes, or rather right behind them within our own minds.'[5]

The Western mystic, Pierre Teilhard de Chardin — a Jesuit priest and eminent scientist — had similar ideas. He believed that, as the mind evolves towards greater complexity, we reach the crucial point of discovering our own evolution. Once this awareness envelops the planet, Teilhard said, we approach the Omega Point, marked by a rise in consciousness, and culminating in a 'spirit of the earth': collective human spirituality.

> *Without stirring abroad*
> *One can know the whole world;*
> *Without looking out of the window*
> *One can see the way of heaven.*
>
>   *(Tao Te Ching)*[6]

Paradoxically, some of the strongest challenges to the mundane world view have come from theoretical physics. Since the mid-1970s, a steady stream of books — such as *The*

Tao of Physics[7], *The Dancing Wu-Li Masters*[8], *Wholeness and The Implicate Order*[9] and *God And The New Physics*[10] — has suggested that we are moving beyond Newton's clockwork universe, towards a world view which looks remarkably mystical.

Quantum physics and relativity transformed Newton's orderly universe into a murky chaos. Our common-sense reality turns out to be a cosy illusion, a sham. The world does not exist 'out there' in the way that we fondly imagined. 'The search for the ultimate stuff of the universe, says Gary Zukav[11], 'ends with the discovery that there isn't any.'

When we look closer and closer at 'solid objects' — such as chairs, candles and chrysanthemums — we do not see tiny but separate particles, but rather an interlocked web of energy fields. The material world seems to have dissolved before our very eyes. Reality, it seems, is a mere trick of the light! As mystics have said for centuries, the world of solid, separate objects is a superficial appearance, 'maya', an illusion. At the quantum level, everything is interconnected. Everything is an interwoven pattern of dancing energy, of light.

What is more, quantum physics has shown that consciousness plays a crucial role in physical reality. There are no observers, only participants. Reality seems to mould itself to our thoughts, beliefs and desires in apparently miraculous ways. Back in 1930, physicist Sir James Jeans noted that '... the universe begins to look more like a great thought than a great machine'.[12]

The new biology[13] is shifting towards a similar vision of reality. Remarkable studies have shown that people, monkeys, rats, birds and even crystals seem to 'communicate' in telepathic-like ways, which the mundane world view would dismiss as impossible. We are not isolated conglomerations of molecules. We are connected to everyone else — and in a way that transcends time and space!

Biologist Rupert Sheldrake — whose revolutionary book *A New Science of Life* was reviewed as 'the best candidate there has been for burning for many years' — emphasises that molecular biology is not false; it merely takes a limited perspective. He compares it to understanding how a television works: traditional biology examines the 'hardware' of the TV set in trying to see how the picture is formed, but ignores the crucial 'software', the invisible wave transmissions.

Perhaps we are moving towards seeing the true 'solid stuff' of the universe as consciousness — expressing itself in a myriad different forms? Perhaps all energy, all matter, is conscious? Perhaps clouds, rocks, trees, birds and elephants are all evolving forms of consciousness? If so — if we are minds-which-happen-to-have-bodies, rather than bodies-which-happen-to-have-minds — then perhaps our consciousness does not *require* a body at all?

There is striking evidence — both anecdotal and experimental — that the 'software' of the mind *can* exist outside the 'hardware' of the brain. The Swiss physician Elisabeth Kübler-Ross, famous for her work on death and dying, reports the case[15] of an architect whose body had been horribly mangled in a car accident on a Swiss mountain pass. The man said that he left his body and found himself floating above the road. The accident was holding up traffic heading for a major football event, and he could hear people cursing and swearing at the delay. Then he heard a woman praying for the victim of the road accident — praying for him. She was praying so fervently, almost frantically, that he decided he would return to his body, with the intention of being able to thank her one day. He 'moved' towards the voice and somehow memorised, in his 'out-of-body' state, the registration number of her car. Three doctors had already pronounced him dead, but miraculously he survived. Several months later, he was able to tell a doctor he trusted about his out-of-body experience, and begged him to find the woman who had prayed. She was traced — and broke down in tears at this confirmation that her prayers had been heard.

If you are trapped in the mundane world view, believing that consciousness somehow evolved from matter, then such tales are nonsense — and will probably be dismissed as fraud, delusion or mere coincidence. Within the old model, anything which exceeds the narrow limits of the five senses and rational thinking simply cannot exist. As John Kenneth Galbraith notes, 'Faced with having to change our views or prove that there is no need to do so, most of us get busy on the proof.'[16]

In Plato's famous allegory of the cave[17], he asks us to imagine people chained inside a dark, underground cave. A fire burns at the entrance, and in its flickering light, shadows of the outside world are projected onto the walls of the cave. The prisoners, immobilised by their chains, can see nothing but these shadows of reality. One day, one of the captives is liberated and dragged out of the cave. At first, he is blinded by the sunlight, but as his vision clears, he is stunned to realise that *this* is the magnificent real world, that the shadows on the wall were mere illusions. The man rushes back to inform the others of his amazing discovery — but they laugh at his crazy tales of the 'real world', and cling relentlessly to their chains.

Perhaps, like Plato's prisoners, we have been chained to the walls of our twentieth century cave, dismissing 'mad tales' of more glorious, expansive visions of reality, and stubbornly insisting that mere shadows are real?

> *If we are only open to those discoveries which*
> *will accord with what we already know, we*
> *might as well stay shut.*
>
> (Alan Watts)[18]

When the explorer Magellan landed on the shores of Tierra del Fuego, the natives greeted the rowing boats which carried the sailors ashore, but were unable to see the sailing ships anchored a little way out to sea. As far as the natives were concerned, it was quite impossible for such huge sailing vessels to exist — and so the ships were invisible to them. Even when a ship was pointed out to them, large as life, they could see only an unbroken horizon.

Those who are blindly committed to their faith in the old world view, believing it to be the 'whole truth and nothing but the truth', are facing a similar dilemma. If you insist that sailing ships cannot exist, then find to your dismay that more and more people report sightings of sailing ships, what do you do? Believe they are all mad, mistaken or merely hallucinating? Cling to those who haven't yet seen a sailing ship? Or do you admit there just might be more things in heaven and earth than you have yet dreamt of?

Within the emerging new vision of reality, what used to be solid, material, unquestionably 'real' — the hard little nuggets of reality — is seen to be elusive, unpredictable, illusory, a chimera. Conversely, the once-dismissed, ethereal aspects of the mundane world view — thoughts, feelings, beliefs, desires, patterns, meaning, significance, information, energy, consciousness — begin to look more and more like the 'solid stuff' of our emerging new world. Where there was once a 'ghost in the machine', it is now the ghost which seems to be more real. A looking glass world indeed!

The old rules still apply, of course — if you drop an apple, it will still fall to the ground. If you crack an egg into a bowl, it will not leap back into its shell and re-seal itself. But we begin to see that our old model robs us of other dimensions of reality. It limits and distorts our vision and potential. It leads us to believe that we are isolated beings in a cold, harsh, empty universe. It deprives us of the meaningful and the miraculous.

The Chinese word for crisis — wei-chi — has two meanings: danger and opportunity. For those who cling to the mundane world view, the coming crisis does indeed mean danger; all our former certainty about the world 'out there' is under threat. But for those who are willing to let go, to break free from their chains, to develop alternative visions, the road ahead is one of unimaginable opportunity and experience.

> *To see a world in a grain of sand,*
> *And a heaven in a wild flower,*
> *Hold infinity in the palm of your hand,*
> *And eternity in an hour.*
>
> *(William Blake)*[19]

As we approach this quantum leap in consciousness, I believe we are shifting from a physical to a metaphysical vision of reality — from matter to energy, from materialism to mentalism, from an inert universe to an evolving, conscious universe. We are beginning to move beyond the limitations of the rational mind, beyond the five senses, beyond space and time, to explore the inner realms, to stretch the boundaries of our consciousness. We are reaching beyond our human potential towards our spiritual potential.

I believe we are on the threshold of a vision which might represent the end of science as we know it — that the boundaries between physics and psychology might dissolve, in the face of a transcendent metaphor that goes far beyond what most scientists have ever dreamt. As the 'New Age' approaches, we are poised to take a giant step beyond our old visions, a dramatic leap from the clifftop.

We are becoming aware — from the very depths of our being — that we do not simply *affect* reality, we *create* it. Every single aspect of it. Our outer world mirrors our inner world. All our explorations of outer space have really been adventures into inner space, dream-like gazes into a holographic mirror. With this flash of insight, we open ourselves to the miraculous.

Already, many seeds of this ancient yet revolutionary idea—that we create our own reality—have been germinating; some are even coming into flower. Quantum physics has not only shown that the mind has impact upon physical reality, but that consciousness is perhaps fundamental to matter. 'Taken to its extreme,' says Paul Davies[20], 'this idea implies that the universe only achieves a concrete existence as a result of this perception — it is created by its own inhabitants!' John Wheeler similarly asks 'May the universe in some strange way be 'brought into being' by the vital act of participation?'[21] And another physicist, Freeman Dyson, says 'I think our consciousness ... is an active agent forcing the molecular complexes to make choices between one quantum state and another. In other words, mind is inherent in every electron ...'[22]

If this sounds like science fiction, consider the curious experiment conducted by physicist Helmut Schmidt.[23]

Schmidt linked up a heat lamp to a random number generator, and placed both in his garden shed. He arranged it so that the heat lamp was turned on and off in a completely random way. In a trial run, as expected, the lamp was on half the time, and off half the time. Schmidt then placed a cat in the shed, during cold weather. To his surprise, he now found that the heat lamp was on far more than it was off, in a way that defied chance. It seemed that the cat — which presumably preferred to be warm — was somehow influencing the random number generator!

If a cat can create its reality in such a way, presumably without 'choosing' to do so, in what ways might we be creating our *own* reality, without any conscious awareness of how or what we are doing? Might it be possible that — as mystics have always suggested — we create every aspect of our physical reality? That the whole universe was, *and is*, created by consciousness?

> *For any speculation which does not at first look crazy, there is no hope.*
>
> *(Freeman Dyson)*[24]

For those who have spiritual beliefs of any kind — who are used to taking a leap of faith — embracing this 'crazy' possibility might come quite easily. After all, we are moving towards a mystical world view: a vision in which consciousness is the primary reality, we are all ultimately One, and reality is an illusion that we create. These are aspects of the perennial philosophy — the ancient wisdom that transcends cultural, scientific and religious dogma — which has been spread by prophets, mystics and visionaries for thousands of years.

According to one NASA scientist, 'For the scientist who

has lived by his faith in the power of reason, the story ends like a bad dream. He has scaled the mountains of ignorance, he is about to conquer the highest peak; and as he pulls himself over the final rock, he is greeted by a band of theologians who have been sitting there for centuries.'[25]

Science and religion — for so long separated by a vast chasm — are moving closer and closer together. The duality is dissolving as the separate visions of reality — from churches and temples, from universities and laboratories — begin to coalesce. However, we will not be simply reverting to ancient mysticism, nor to a pre-technological way of life. The new world view is not a step into the past, but a *synergy* of old and new.

> *Over the peak spreading clouds,*
> *At its source the river's cold.*
> *If you would see,*
> *Climb the mountain top.*
>
> *(Hakuyo)*[26]

A metaphysical world view suggests that our three-dimensional reality is a mere projection of a higher, multidimensional reality; like prisoners in Plato's cave, we mistake our complex holographic illusions for reality. (Quantum physics, similarly, suggests there might be 10^{89} dimensions or more.[27]) Animals can see and hear things which we cannot — so is it so strange to imagine that there might be other dimensions of reality which we do not ordinarily perceive?

Our conscious mind might be compared with a radio which picks up several stations. The 'station' of physical reality is the loudest, so that most of the time we do not hear the more subtle stations, and are perhaps unaware they exist. But if we hush this noisy station — for example, through meditation — other stations can be heard more clearly. As psychologist William James suggests, 'Our normal waking consciousness, rational consciousness as we call it, is but one special type of consciousness, while all about it, parted from it by the filmiest of screens, there lie potential forms of consciousness entirely different.'[28]

We all know that our most creative ideas — flashes of intuition, unexpected solutions, 'lateral thinking' — come unbidden, while our rational mind is out of the way; when we are daydreaming, listening to music, soaking in the bath, driving along a mesmerising highway. The great scientific breakthroughs have not come through painstaking logic, but from inspirational dreams and sudden intuitions: visions of what may be. Einstein reported that his original ideas were rarely conceived in words; his special theory of relativity arose from imagining a ride on a lightbeam. The chemist Kekulé realised that benzene has a ring-like structure through his famous dream of a snake holding its own tall. Perhaps such visions come to us from higher dimensions of reality?

> *Sell your cleverness and buy bewilderment;*
> *Cleverness is mere opinion, bewilderment is*
> *intuition.*
>
> *(Jalal-uddin Rumi)*[29]

CHANNELLING
Let us now take another leap — what if there were other *conscious beings* in the higher dimensions of reality? It would perhaps be very surprising if there were not. It would be a supreme arrogance to assume that ours is the only dimension in which conscious minds exist! This would

be like insisting that, amidst a physical universe of billions of galaxies, there is only life on Earth.

So, if there *are* conscious beings in 'higher' realms, might it be possible that they could communicate with us? Perhaps we seem to have strayed into science fiction again — but in the past twenty years, there has been a massive increase in the number of people claiming to be 'channelling' beings from higher dimensions, and before we dismiss them as self-deluding cranks, perhaps we should suspend disbelief and remember that it is only when we go *beyond* what we already know that we make new discoveries.

Channelling has an ancient history, and whatever our beliefs about the phenomenon — whether we see it as communication with beings from other dimensions, as split-off portions of the subconscious mind, as dipping into the collective unconscious, or as an expression of the multidimensional nature of the self — the fact remains that some channelled material reveals astonishing wisdom and knowledge. The most advanced sources of the new vision of reality are undoubtedly, to my mind, channelled teachings — some of which make our white-collared priests and white-coated scientists look like well-meaning simpletons.

The Seth books, for example, have sold millions of copies. Seth describes himself as 'an energy personality essence no longer focused in physical reality'. His channel, American writer Jane Roberts, describes how Seth first communicated through her, while she sat at her desk: 'What happened next was like a 'trip' without drugs. If someone had slipped me an LSD cube on the sly, the experience couldn't have been more bizarre ... It was as if the physical world were really tissue-paper thin, hiding infinite dimensions of reality, and I was suddenly flung through the tissue paper with a huge ripping sound. My body sat at the table, my hands furiously scribbling down the words and ideas that flashed through my head ....'[30] What emerged was an extraordinary manuscript entitled *The Physical Universe As Idea Construction.*

Within a few months, Seth was speaking directly through Jane — as he did for the next twenty years — with a curious accent which has been variously called Russian, Dutch, Irish, German, Italian and French. With a characteristic personality, intellect and humour of his own, Seth consistently denied being an aspect of Jane's subconscious.

> *I am no misty-eyed ghostly spirit, materialising*
> *in the middle of the night. I am simply an*
> *intelligent personality no longer bound by your*
> *physical laws ...*
>
> *(Seth)*[31]

In 1965, Helen Cohn Shucman, a New York psychologist and atheist, began to hear an inner voice which urged her to take notes. Fearing she was going crazy, she tried to ignore it, but it persisted — and she eventually found that the 'voice' wished to dictate a book. In 1975, the massive three-volume text, *A Course In Miracles*, was published. Although Christian (and unfortunately sexist) in language, this profound and moving textbook-manual on finding inner peace has reached the hearts of Christians and non-Christians alike. To date, it has sold more than half a million copies.

Mary-Margaret Moore was under medical hypnosis for back pain when she unexpectedly found herself in a past life — and the energy vortex which has become known as 'Bartholomew' spoke through her for the first time. In the year that followed, she often panicked over whether her channelling might be harmful. 'I was afraid that I was operating under some grand ego illusion that would end up plunging me into a karmic mess that would take lifetimes to pull out of.' Eventually, however, she realised that the information given by Bartholomew was wise, loving and immensely helpful — and more than a decade (and three books) later, she is still channelling Bartholomew.

Sanaya Roman had been receiving messages through a Ouija board for a year when, in 1977, she asked for the 'highest possible guide and teacher' to come through — and Orin introduced himself. For the following four years, Sanaya channelled another being, Dan, while she began to attune to Orin's higher vibrations. During this period, 'Orin could only come through on the Ouija board, as was apparent when I tried to let him come through me and almost passed out. At first I felt like I was expanding from top to bottom, becoming sponge-like, larger than the room, but still encased in an energy field. I felt a crushing sensation in my chest, and a sense of power and love.'[33] Since 1981, she has channelled Orin directly — and the results have helped thousands to transform their lives.

In 1974, Jach Pursel, a business executive in Florida, 'dozed off' while meditating — and his wife Peny found herself talking to a disembodied consciousness which came to be known as Lazaris. Lazaris (pronounced La-*zar*-is) describes himself as a 'spark of consciousness', a multidimensional being who — unlike most channelled sources — has never occupied a physical body.

On the first audiotape I ever heard of Lazaris, he is introduced by the soft-spoken American accent of his channel, Jach Pursel. There is a brief pause while Jach 'gets out of the way' to allow Lazaris through — and then a strange voice begins to speak, with a unique accent once described by the channel as Chaucerian Middle English, though linguists have said that it combines a multitude of different accents. The accent has remained consistent throughout the fifteen years that Jach has been channelling Lazaris — as have the humour, warmth, love, incredible knowledge and wisdom that Lazaris communicates.

Lazaris compares the process of channelling with a television broadcast — and just as newscasters are not inside the television set, Lazaris stresses that 'he' is never inside Jach's body. '... we connect energies that are thoughts into a system of vibration that we then transmit through the cosmos and the various levels. The system of vibration then enters your reality through the Mental Plane, then drifts down, in its way, to the Physical Plane — much as a television signal to the antenna — and then is amplified and comes out of the vocal cords, the mouth, and the speaking structure of that which is the Channel.'[34]

Psychologist Jon Klimo has written a comprehensive study of channelling: its history, the channelled 'entities', the messages, the possible explanations. In seeking a way of understanding channelling, he asks, 'what if our own respective minds are really part of some vast impersonal sea of mind (or energy) with which we interact to give birth to further, seemingly separate minds or personalities ...?'[35] Channelling, he suggests, is the ability to connect one dimension of the implicate-order sea of consciousness with another, in spite of the differing frequencies of vibration involved — rather like tapping into Sheldrake's 'M-field', or Russell's 'Gaiafield', but across different dimensions of reality.[36]

In summarising the *content* of messages from channelled sources, Klimo notes the astonishing uniformity of their perspectives on reality. Whoever these sources are, they are in remarkable agreement with one another. Moreover, some seem better informed about the cutting edge of science than our top scientists! The sources also confirm that the sudden surge in channelling marks the dawning of a new age — that humanity is at a turning point, the threshold of a new era of consciousness.

> You live in a loving universe.
> *All of the forces are here to give you assistance,*
> *to give you support.*
>
> (*Emmanuel*)[37]

If we wait for conventional science to declare that such messages are 'genuine', we might drum our fingers forever; in the meantime, an invaluable source of wisdom, with the potential to transform our everyday lives, would be ignored. Perhaps it is enough to realise that channelled sources offer a picture of reality which is strikingly consistent with ancient wisdom and the new science — and to open our hearts and minds, and listen.

Of course, it is crucial that we are sceptical and discerning about channelled sources — that we think and question for ourselves. Just because a source claims to be disembodied does not mean that it is all-knowing. (Indeed, the majority of messages received via mediums from those who have 'died' suggest that death, in itself, does not raise one's IQ in the slightest!) Moreover, channelling is wide open to fraud, cranks and self-deception.

Perhaps a good rule of thumb is to pay less attention to the reputed source than to the *depth* and *quality* of information provided, when deciding whether to accept or reject it. Is it consistent? Is it helpful? Is it wise? Is it practical? Is it joyful and expansive? Does it feel intuitively right, even if it contradicts our 'common-sense' notions of reality? How might it be used to change our lives?

2
Beyond the Bridge of Belief

*This world is full of miracles. They stand in
shining silence next to every dream of pain and
suffering, of sin and guilt. They are the dream's
alternative, the choice to be the dreamer, rather
than deny the active role in making up the
dream.*

(A Course In Miracles)[1]

There is a Zen story of a university professor who came
to enquire about the philosophy of Zen. While the Zen
master Nan-in silently prepared tea, the professor ex-
pounded on his own beliefs at some length. Nan-in began
to pour tea into his visitor's cup — and carried on pouring.
The cup overflowed, and still Nan-in poured, until the
professor exclaimed 'It is already full! No more will go in!'
'Like this cup', explained Nan-in, 'you are already full of your
own opinions and speculations. How can I show you Zen
unless you first empty your cup?'

Each of us has a cup full of beliefs about the nature of
reality — whether or not we are aware of it. For most of us,
the cup is already overflowing with the mundane world
view: our faith in scientists and experts, our conviction that
the universe is a meaningless accident, that consciousness
somehow evolved from matter, our belief that there is an
objective reality which is gradually being discovered. We
are reluctant to abandon our faith. The new vision holds
the promise of personal and social transformation — but only
if we are prepared to 'empty our cup' and listen.

So — what are the messages which channelled sources so urgently wish us to hear? What is the new vision of reality which they have come to teach?

1. Consciousness creates matter

According to the mundane world view, our consciousness is a curious quirk of nature which evolved — due to random genetic mutations — from the 'solid stuff' which makes up the universe. Mystics, on the other hand, have always said that consciousness came first, that matter is an expression of the divine Mind. Fritjof Capra[2] says that we cannot expect science, at its present stage of development, to either confirm or contradict such a viewpoint. But channelled sources are quite explicit and firm: we create every aspect of our physical reality.

Seth, along with other sources, tells us that consciousness *creates* matter. 'Your scientists are finally learning ... that mind can influence matter. They still have to discover the fact that mind *creates* and forms matter.'[3] In other words, consciousness brings atoms and molecules into being. Consciousness is not an emergent property of matter, but its very creator!

> *Do you realise that your physical world is illusion? That it is in reality built of light? That your physical body, if you could but see it with clear vision, is composed of light?*
>
> *(White Eagle)*[4]

Lazaris[5] explains that subatomic particles are 'trapped light' — light moving in a spiral, either clockwise or anticlockwise. The only difference between the atoms of a chair and those of a giraffe lies in the frequency of vibration of the particles. Everything is trapped light, vibrating at various frequencies.

Light, as we know, is energy, and the source of energy — as the new physics seems to be on the brink of discovering — is *consciousness*.

Thought creates energy creates light creates trapped light creates atoms and molecules. Consciousness creates matter!

2. We create our own reality

Not only do we bring atoms and molecules into being, but — according to metaphysics — we choreograph their dance. Since consciousness is the source of everything, nothing happens unless we *make* it happen. Our thoughts decide which of an infinite number of possible and probable events will actually manifest in *our* reality. Thus, metaphysics says that *nothing* happens by chance. We create (or allow) each and every event of our lives. There are no exceptions. As Lazaris puts it, there is no asterisk, no small print, no hidden meanings: we create it all.

We create every success, every failure, every illness, every relationship, every promotion, every piece of good or bad 'luck', every family row, every problem, every trauma, every 'accident', everything. There are no triumphs or tragedies other than those that we create. Each of us is the source of all our suffering and all our joy. Our problems are not caused by the world 'out there' — nor by God, fate or karma — but by our inner world. Each and every moment of our lives is created (or allowed) by our own beliefs, attitudes, thoughts, feelings, choices, desires and expectations.

> *The stuff of which you are made is so charged with the ability to create that everything you touch comes to life: every thought, every iden-tity, every image.*
>
> *(The Starseed Transmissions)*[6]

Let us be clear that this is just as dramatic and revolutionary as it sounds. It is not just another version of positive thinking'. It is not suggesting that we merely *influence* the world 'out there', but that everyday reality only exists in the precise form that we create it — through our own conscious beliefs, attitudes and expectations.

Beliefs create experience, not vice versa. If our house is burgled, for example, we created that reality. It didn't just 'happen' to us. We *made* it happen. We attracted it into our lives, because it reflects an aspect of our inner world. Perhaps we believe the world is a dangerous place, that you're not even safe in your own home, that people are basically greedy, that we live in a bad neighbourhood, or feel guilty about our material possessions .... Whatever the reasons, our task is to *learn* from the experience — not to allow it to reinforce the beliefs which made it happen in the first place, but to learn about ourselves, and to realise that our thoughts do create reality.

Channelled sources are clear that 'creating our own reality' is not meant symbolically. It is quite literal. Our external reality faithfully reflects our inner world: 'The change of thoughts, feelings and beliefs into physical, objectively perceived phenomena is as natural as water changing into ice, for example, or a caterpillar turning into a butterfly' says Seth.[7] If we expect life to be full of pain and suffering, we will make it so. If we expect life to abound with love, joy and laughter, then that is the 'probable reality' we will create. From their own perspective, optimists and pessimists are both correct. Life is a self-fulfilling prophecy.

Of course, our limited rational mind — which believes in the mundane world view — sees such ideas as quite crazy. Of course the world is real and solid! Of course we are victims of luck and fate! After all, if we create our own reality, why are we not aware of it? How can we convince ourselves that life comes up with surprises, that events simply 'happen to us'?

One reason is that, on the physical plane, our thoughts and beliefs do not 'manifest' immediately. For example, the firm belief that we will be offered a wonderful new job might be planted a year or so before it actually happens so when it does, we tell ourselves we have been lucky, or it was meant to happen.

In the world of spirit — as in the world of dreams — every thought manifests instantly. We imagine a bubbling brook in a lush green meadow, and suddenly here it is! We imagine fire-breathing dragons chasing us, and they appear! In the non-physical realms, *as on earth*, we create our own reality, according to our beliefs and expectations. As above, so below. Those who expect to be greeted by St. Peter at the pearly gates after death will experience this, while those who believe they have been wicked might at first create their own fire-and-brimstone hell.

However, in the physical world — thanks to the illusion of time — beliefs create reality quite slowly, giving us an opportunity to learn how to control psychic energy, to consciously take charge of our thoughts and beliefs, in order to create the realities that we want, to *learn* how to create a heaven on earth.

> *Time is the cushion between the thoughts you*
> *think and the realities those thoughts produce ...*
> *Time gives you space to make mistakes.*
>
> (Lazaris)[8]

As we approach the twenty-first century, this process of

reality creation is said to be speeding up — hence the breathtaking pace of recent sociopolitical changes. On the negative side, this means that we must be more vigilant about our thoughts; we might create 'fire-breathing dragons' quite rapidly these days! On the positive side, it means that we can now create wondrous realities, personally and globally, in a short space of time: there are no limitations other than those we choose to believe in.

But how is it *logistically* possible that each of us creates our own reality? Don't our different realities contradict each other? Metaphysics suggests that we each write our own play, and then act as magnets for those who will fit into our script — as long as *we* fit *their* script. Like attracts like. If we expect to be badly treated, we attract those who will mistreat us. If we expect people to be warm and loving, we meet those who confirm our expectations. The parts mesh together in a breathtakingly intricate way, since *everyone* we meet (or even hear about) forms part of our script — including 'bit players' such as the shop assistant who sells you a loaf of bread — yet the scripts are always consistent. Fortunately, we can re-write our scripts. If the people in our lives change, it is because *we* have decided to change. We might even feel drawn towards a new city, a different profession or another country, in which we will now feel more at home.

Collectively, it is said that we even produce such global phenomena as weather and natural disasters: 'You each participate in the creation of each thunderstorm, each new spring, each flood, earthquake, and summer rain' says Seth.[9] The weather is said to reflect the feelings and beliefs of the individuals in that particular area. Lazaris suggests that this is why earthquakes and hurricanes never cause major devastation in such areas as New York and San Francisco;

the people who live there simply value themselves and their property too highly!

3. We live many, many lifetimes

We are eternal beings, who existed 'before' we were born and will exist 'after' we die. In Seth's words, you are as dead now as you will ever be! 'I am telling you that you are not a cosmic bag of bones and flesh, thrown together through some mixture of chemicals and elements ...'[10] We adopt bodies, he suggests, in the same way that a space traveller wears a spacesuit — and for much the same reasons.[11]

Channelled sources consistently state that we live many physical lifetimes, as well as experiencing other dimensions of reality. Such a doctrine may seem anathema to those of us brought up in the Judeo-Christian tradition, which teaches that we only have one lifetime in which to grow and develop. Yet there is a great deal of well-documented anecdotal evidence of people recalling one or more 'past lives', providing accurate details which often defy logical explanation,[12] and reincarnation explains many otherwise puzzling phenomena, such as children with extraordinary gifts or wisdom, feeling we have known someone before, or déjà vu experiences. At a purely rational level, reincarnation seems to make sense.

Many illustrious Westerners have believed in reincarnation: Plato, Socrates, Julius Caesar, Pythagoras, Goethe, Nietzsche, Immanuel Kant, William Blake, Yeats, Coleridge, Shelley, Balzac, Tennyson, Browning, Mahler, Wagner, Tolstoy, Napoleon Bonaparte, Thomas Edison, Walt Whitman, Louisa May Alcott, Salvador Dali, Sir Arthur Conan Doyle, Benjamin Franklin, Lloyd George — to name but a few.

Moreover, there is evidence that reincarnation was

taught in early Christianity, but that the doctrine was declared heresy by a church council in the sixth century A.D., on purely *political* grounds. (Lazaris suggests that people were deemed less likely to rob, murder and pillage if they believed they only had one lifetime in which to gain their salvation!) The Bible was amended accordingly, but traces of the early doctrine do reman in the New Testament: 'Except a man be born again, he cannot see the kingdom of God'; 'And no man ascended up to heaven, but he that came down from heaven.' More directly, Jesus said, '... that Elias is come already, and they knew him not ...' Then the disciples understood that He spake to them of John the Baptist.' (Matthew 17: 12-13.) Jesus also seemed to refer to the law of karma: '... for all they that take the sword shall perish with the sword.' (Matthew 26: 52.)

> *Our birth is but a sleep and a forgetting;*
> *The Soul that rises with us, our life's Star,*
> *Hath had elsewhere its setting,*
> *And cometh from afar.*
> *Not in entire forgetfulness,*
> *And not in utter nakedness,*
> *But trailing clouds of glory do we come*
> *From God who is our home.*
>   *(William Wordsworth)[13]*

According to Seth, 'You will reincarnate whether or not you believe that you will. It is much easier if your theories fit reality, but if they do not, then you do not change the nature of reincarnation one iota.'[14] On the other hand, the Old Age view of reincarnation — that we live one life after another, until we eventually achieve enlightenment, and are freed from the physical plane — now looks like a children's fairy tale: a vastly simplified version of a much more complex reality.

Each of us, it is said, experiences tens or hundreds of lifetimes — as both sexes, in each of the races of the world, and in each major historical period — and these lifetimes are concurrent. It isn't that 'in a past life' you were, say, a peasant farmer in medieval France, but that that aspect of you is *still* growing crops. It is only that your consciousness is *now* tuned in to the frequency of this 'current' life in the late twentieth century — your 'previous' life might have been as a computer programmer in the twenty-third century!

As Einstein discovered, time is an illusion. There is only the eternal now. Everything we have ever experienced — and will ever experience — is occurring, in some dimension of reality, at this moment. All events of history — past and future — are happening 'now.' The construction of the Pyramids, the birth of Mozart, the American Civil War, and the first space-travel beyond our solar system are all happening *right now*. All that moves is our consciousness.

Our different reincarnational selves are not rungs up the ladder of time, but more like pieces in a giant jigsaw puzzle. We exist *right now* in a multitude of dimensions. We are simply so hypnotised, so fascinated, by our 'current' physical reality that we are not aware of these other dimensions — although it is possible, through 'altered states of consciousness' (meditation, visualisation, hypnosis and so on) to obtain glimpses of these other states. Occasionally, too, we might experience 'bleedthroughs' from our simultaneous lives: perhaps in dreams, fantasies, sudden impulses, disconnected images, an interest in a certain country or historical period, or calling someone by another name.

I have been here before,
But when or how I cannot tell.
I know the grass beyond the door,
The sweet keen smell,
The sighing sound, the lights around the shore.
                    (Dante Gabriel Rossetti)[15]

What is more, each soul is part of a group entity. Lazaris, for example, always refers to himself as 'we' — not, he says humorously, out of any sense of imperiousness, but because he experiences himself as many different selves. Seth, likewise, says that every soul is a group of selves, or a soul within the 'oversoul' — and each oversoul forms just part of a multidimensional personality structure. (Occasionally, another 'aspect' of Seth — know as Seth Two — would be channelled through Jane Roberts. Seth Two had never incarnated in physical form, and said that 'I am the Seth that is beyond the Seth that you know. And in me the knowledge and vitality of that Seth still rings. In your terms, I am a future Seth ...'[16])

Channelled sources suggest that it is merely a convenient fiction to say that we live one life at a time. In fact, we not only have simultaneous lives in other periods of history, but may also have one or two 'parallel selves' who are alive now, in the 1990s — same time, different space. Or we might have overlapping lives, in which we are born in one life several months or years before we 'die' in another life.

The picture becomes even more complicated by the notion of probable selves. According to the new metaphysics, we are just one of an infinity of probable selves — our counterparts in other systems of reality. Imagine that you had a strong urge to become a dancer when you were a teenager but eventually decided to be an architect instead.

When you made this decision, another 'probable self' was born which *did* become a dancer, with a conscious mind just like yours, in a world just as 'real' and physical as our own — and *that* probable self would look on you as a probable self! With every decision, new probable selves split off into other probable universes, developing all the possibilities which we turned our back on.

Such a viewpoint might wildly stretch our imagination — but the concept of 'probable universes' has been discussed by theoretical physicists for the past thirty years, in the many worlds interpretation of quantum mechanics. Reality seems to be inconceivably complex.

4. The present moment is our point of power

The idea that every event is simultaneous might lead us to conclude that free will is an illusion. After all, if our future is already happening, how can we choose what we will do next? Surely the choice has already been made. But a recurrent theme of metaphysics is that, *right now*, we have the power of choice. Nothing is predestined. This present moment, where our consciousness is focused, is our point of power, in which we may choose to spiral off into one or another of our 'probable futures'. We do have both freedom and responsibility; and since time is an illusion, it follows that we should equally have the power to change *past* events. Channelled sources do support this crazy-sounding conclusion — we can change not only our future, but also our past!

At all times, we have freedom of choice. At a soul level, we choose to be born. We carefully choose our parents, the circumstances of our childhood, and perhaps a few significant life events. Our family, friends and lovers will often be people we have known in other lives, and have chosen to meet again. Our best friend today might be our mother, son, husband and neighbour in other lives. We also choose our children — who are often more mature souls who come as our teachers.

Similarly, we choose when to die. No-one can leave the physical plane without the consent of their Higher Self. Thus, deaths by road accident, heart disease, train crashes, cancer, cot deaths, deliberate overdoses, and even murder, are all 'deaths by suicide' *at a higher level*. Death is but a willing and joyful transition of awareness. It is only a tragedy for those left behind. (Perhaps this is one reason why we invariably feel angry with someone who has died; we know, at a deep level, that they *chose* to leave us.)

> *The moment of death is also a moment of remembering. I cannot tell you how often you dear ones have left your bodies and begun to laugh.*
>
> *(Emmanuel)*[17]

5. We are here to learn, grow and have fun

If we choose the circumstances of each lifetime, one might wonder why on earth anyone decides to be born into a Third World country which faces poverty and famine; or to parents who are cruel, violent and abusive. Why don't we all simply choose to have a good time?

Some would say it is due to the law of karma. Karma has been called the law of cause and effect, or law of divine retribution: 'As ye sow, so shall ye reap.' The idea is that, if you suffer in this lifetime, it is karmic payment for your misdeeds in 'past' lifetimes. If you are poor, it is because you lacked compassion for the poor; if you suffer violence, it is because you have been violent.

It doesn't take much imagination to see how such a

doctrine might be abused. 'Oh, they're only starving because they were wicked in times past. We'd better leave them to their karma!' And indeed, channelled sources suggest that the law of karma *was* distorted for political ends — as a way of mollifying the poor and oppressed, and justifying social inequality.

The new understanding of karma is that we create our own karma; it is a personal choice. Every thought and action does have consequences — but it isn't that God, or anyone else, sends us back to Earth with karmic debts to pay. We decide *for ourselves* what circumstances, relationships or events will help us to learn and to grow. If all lives are simultaneous, it would be absurd to suggest that our suffering is caused by our past mistakes. There is no past! Karma is not punishment or reward, but an opportunity to grow, to become more of who we are.

In order to experience every aspect of the physical plane, we might all choose to be beggars and thieves, to suffer from disease, and to die violent deaths — as well as choosing to be rich and powerful, to be parents, to lead religious lives, and to develop our own unique talents. In different lifetimes, we work on different aspects of ourselves.

Lazaris, Seth and others say that there are no karmic debts to pay *unless we believe it to be so* — and that we only carry negative influences from other lifetimes if we choose to do so. We are never at the mercy of our 'past' lives. We can simply release ourselves from the past by choosing to learn what we need to learn. Our past — in this and other lifetimes — might influence, but it never controls us.

> *Spirit is in a state of grace forever.*
> *Your reality is only spirit.*
> *Therefore you are in a state of grace forever.*
>   *(A Course In Miracles)*[18]

So what is the meaning or purpose of life? Why are we here? What does personal growth really mean? Lazaris repeatedly says that there are two primary purposes in life: to learn how to have fun, and to consciously create success ... What, no pain and suffering? No struggle and conflict? No blood and gore? No rosaries and hairshirts? No — according to Lazaris, life was never meant to be difficult; we have simply chosen to make it so! Our purpose is to learn how to enjoy life, to fulfil our potential, to love ourselves and others, to be joyful.

Life is not just about getting through the days, hoping we might have some good luck and happiness along the way. It is a marvellous adventure, a voyage of self-discovery, a magically creative process. Each and every day provides opportunities to learn, to grow, to expand, to become more of who we are.

If we struggle to become what our Ego sees as 'perfect', inner peace will forever elude us. Bartholomew says 'Your life has been based on the supposition that there is something wrong with you that you've got to fix. I would like to suggest that there is nothing wrong with you, and you certainly don't need to be fixed. Your inner tension comes from *not loving* certain parts of yourself ... When you finally stop trying to be perfect, things will happen.'[19]

Similarly, Seth suggests that we should never aim to be perfect. 'Perfection is not being, for all being is in a state of becoming. This does not mean that all being is in a state of becoming *perfect*, but in a state of becoming more *itself*.[20] Our uniqueness is our gift to the world. All we have to do is to become ourselves.

Spiritual growth does not mean being holier-than-thou. It does not mean meditating for eight hours a day, eating only brown rice and taking a vow of abstinence. It means living life to the full. It means being loving, caring and intimate. It means being self-aware and responsible. It means becoming all that we can be. As Bartholomew[21] says, 'Enlightened ones are rarely very holy. In fact, they are often so outrageous that people look on them as crazy. They do what they *are moved* to do, and leave you to deal with your reaction to it. They have the capacity to just *be human*'. They have awakened from the dream.

6.   We are responsible for our world — personally and globally

If the world is a mirror of our inner selves, this raises serious questions about political and social reform. Must inner reform precede — even replace — social reform? Should we perhaps abandon all thought of helping one another, or trying to change the world? Sadly, some have interpreted metaphysics in this way — but a philosophy which pivots around love, empowerment and responsibility could never advocate turning our back on suffering.

Metaphysics always *gives* us responsibility; it never takes it away. It urges us to *act*, to *love*, to *care*, to *realise* our personal and global visions of the future. Social apathy and indifference has no place in New Age thinking.

If we become aware of, say, famine in Ethiopia or child sexual abuse, then we have chosen to do so — perhaps as an opportunity to be aware of our connectedness with those people, or to express our compassion actively, or to recognise ways in which we are 'starving' or 'abusing' ourselves or others — and *they* might be suffering in order to allow *us* to grow. As soon as we are aware of a problem, we are part of that problem — and we can choose to take loving and responsible action.

It is dangerous nonsense to say that because we create

our own reality, there is no such thing as a 'victim', so we should leave well alone. Until people are *aware* that they create their own reality, they are indeed victims. If someone is starving, or has been abused, their immediate need is for food and the means of growing crops, or for a loving home and sympathetic counsellor — not for metaphysics!

The only caveat to sociopolitical action is that if we see a world we dislike — a world full of suffering, hatred, violence, greed, poverty and oppression — we are, first of all, gazing at our own reflection. The world is a mirror. So we should *also* be healing ourselves. We should *also* be developing self-awareness and self-love. 'Work on yourself and serve the world' said the Grail Knights. Our first responsibility is to know and love ourselves.

This is not a way of evading social responsibility, since a crucial aspect of personal and spiritual growth is *actively* caring about our planet, *actively* expressing our Oneness. Inner change and outer change, like yin and yang, are complementary aspects of the same whole.

However, 'helping' which is motivated by guilt, fear, anger, resentment, self-righteousness, boredom or self-hatred invariably turns out merely to hinder. It perpetuates its own motivation, and cannot have a positive impact. We will not ensure peace by hating war, but rather by loving peace, understanding our 'enemies', and believing in a peaceful world. Hence our need to balance social action with inner healing.

> *Driven by the force of love the fragments of the world seek each other that the world may come into being.*
>
> (Pierre Teilhard de Chardin)[22]

Whenever we reach out to touch the world, our driving forces should be love, hope, joy, trust and empowerment — so that we help people to help themselves to discover their own power, their own capacity to love and respect themselves, their own hope for the future. We will then truly help and inspire them. We will then play a role, each in our own unique way, in co-creating a visionary new world. The twenty-first century is not in 'their' hands, but in ours.

As Bartholomew puts it, 'If you really want to help, quit the talking, quit the thinking, and begin the loving.'[23] Lazaris, similarly, suggests that spiritual growth always starts with love: 'We want to teach people how to learn to love themselves, then how to love others, then how to love their world. Always begin with love.'[24]

7. We are co-creators with God/dess

A recurrent theme of the new spirituality is that we are 'co-creators with God'. God might be referred to as The Force, The Universe, The Light, All That Is, or some other term — but the concept remans of an everchanging, evolving and loving Source which is both transcendent and immanent; a force which Seth says 'is indeed aware of each sparrow that falls, for it *is* each sparrow that falls.'[25] A spark of God/dess is within everything — every person, every spider, every rock, every cloud. Each of us is a fragment of this universal energy, and we create our reality — whether consciously or unconsciously — *with* and *through* God/dess.

The concept of God has so many negative connotations that it is easy to see 'Him' as the invincible tyrant which Nietzsche rightly said must be killed. He has been linked with religious dogma and ritual, guilt, repression, self-denial, sacrifice, patriarchy, vengeance, tyranny and even wars fought in His name. 'You have the image of an old man with a white beard sitting upon some sort of cloud, destroying cities when he feels like it, and doing all those dastardly things that the Old Testament rather attributes to his name' says Lazaris[26] — and as a result, we have thrown out the concept of God altogether. Rather than decide that our *images* of God might have been mere projections, or child-like fancies which need to progress to maturity, many of us decide that, in our clockwork universe, God isn't necessary at all: 'Don't call us, we'll call you!'

However, even scientists are reconsidering the existence of God. (What is the quest for the Grand Unified Force if not the search for God?) Sir Fred Hoyle proposed there is mathematical evidence that the universe was designed by a cosmic intelligence.[27] Physicist Paul Davies[28] says 'It is hard to resist the impression that the present structure of the universe ... has been rather carefully thought out.' And Rupert Sheldrake[29] raises the possibility of a 'transcendent conscious being' who might be the source of the universe.

Capra[30] notes that 'An increasing number of scientists are aware that mystical thought provides a consistent and relevant philosophical background to the theories of contemporary science; a conception of the world in which the scientific discoveries of men and women can be in perfect harmony with their spiritual aims and religious beliefs.'

Although channelled sources acknowledge the 'Christ consciousness' which entered such great spiritual teachers as Jesus and Buddha, the God/dess of the new spirituality is an all-encompassing, conscious energy which transcends the patriarchal images of the Old Age religions. Metaphysics is not necessarily an *alternative* to being, say, Christian, Buddhist or Jewish. It is compatible with any nonfundamentalist spiritual path, since it shares the wisdom and truth which lie at the heart of all the old religions.

> *Like the bee gathering honey from different*
> *flowers, the wise man accepts the essence of*
> *different Scriptures and sees only the good in all*
> *religions.*
>
> (Srimad Bhagavatam)[31]

The new spirituality goes beyond rigid doctrine, beyond sectarianism, beyond the concept of one true religion. It recognises the suffocating restrictions of dogma. It expands *around* and *within* the perennial philosophy. It urges us to think for ourselves, to discover our own inner knowing, in an ever-changing and expanding way — rather than swallowing every word of ancient, culture-bound texts in a way that abnegates personal responsibility.

Moreover, metaphysics is not merely an interesting backcloth to life, a Sunday morning ritual or a conversation piece for dinner parties — but a practical spirituality which can change every moment of our lives, transforming a humdrum routine into a magical world full of love, laughter and joy. By learning how to become *conscious* 'co-creators with God/dess', life can become whatever we desire and imagine, whatever we truly want it to be.

> *A new time is before your species, a time of*
> *realisation, fulfilment and adventure. Accept this*
> *time. Move into it. Dance in the momentum of*
> *its inevitability. It is the breath of Life and the*
> *song of God that you have been cut off from for*
> *so long.*
>
> (The Starseed Transmissions)[32]

THE FUTURE

Many are forecasting that humanity is on the brink of self-destruction. Prophecies of doom and gloom abound. Nostradamus, the Book of Revelations, and countless other mystics and clairvoyants have been cited as evidence that the end of the world is nigh — that the Battle of Armageddon is at hand. Predictions of nuclear warfare, ecological disasters, a shift of the Earth's axis, or giant meteors colliding with the planet in 1999 can be found on almost every bookstall.

Channelled sources agree that we are at a watershed, that the 1990s is the most crucial decade in the whole history of our planet. They too seem divided into pessimists and optimists (which shows that we must be wary of taking disembodied spirits on trust!). However, the more impressive channelled sources — whose knowledge, wisdom and perspective seem to far transcend our own — suggest that the doom-and-gloom merchants are simply playing on our doubts and fears, and that we *can* look forward to the twenty-first century. After all, we create our own reality!

As Lazaris puts it, the problem is not that there will be no future; the problem is that there *will* be a future — and we will be responsible for it. Although many of the pessimists will choose to create their *own* doomsday, the reason why prophecies do not extend into the twenty-first century is that predictions will no longer be accurate in the New Age, because we will be *consciously* creating our own reality. We will no longer be 'victims' of a world which seems beyond our control. The Battle of Armageddon, then, will perhaps be the symbolic conflict between the old and new visions of reality?

*If you learn only one thing in this lifetime, let it
be this: you are responsible for creating your
own happiness.*

                                              (Bartholomew)[33]

If we do indeed create our own reality in order to learn and
grow, we must have collectively created the current global
crisis. We must all be responsible for such looming threats
as the greenhouse effect, radioactive waste, nuclear prolif-
eration, Third World debts, disappearing topsoil and the
AIDS virus. So why might we have created such overwhelming problems? What are the lessons we hope to learn?

Perhaps the purpose or significance of the global crisis
is to force us to shift to the new vision of reality? The
current problems cannot be resolved unless we learn to see
ourselves as globally interconnected, as ultimately One.
Nor can they be resolved by our usual linear-analytic
methods of problem-solving; visionary new approaches
will be required. What is more, a radical revision of our
sociopolitical values is essential, if we are to avoid being
irrevocably lured into the spider's web of ever-increasing
technological and economic growth. We have attempted,
to our cost, to become 'bigger, fatter, shinier acorns'. It is
time for us to grow into oak trees.

According to mysticism, enlightenment stems from
turning our perception upside-down, breaking through our
culture-bound ways of seeing, transcending the limitations
of ordinary awareness. 'What is isn't, and what isn't is.' In
the New Age, our perceptions will be reversed at a cultural
rather than individual level: a *collective* awakening, in
which we begin to 'see through' consensus reality, rather
than 'seeing' through it.

As in Alice's Looking-Glass World, everything will come

to seem topsy-turvy. What was once plain and obvious will be seen as uncertain or illusory. The objective world will start to look shadowy and unreal, while subjective reality will seem more and more of a powerhouse. Instead of implicitly believing in what a scientist sees down a microscope, we will begin to trust more and more in our inner eye.

What once seemed to be irreconcilable opposites — science and religion, analysis and synthesis, rationality and intuition, West and East, materialism and spirituality, yang and yin, conscious and subconscious, objective and subjective, individual and society — will be seen to be complementary aspects of a greater whole. The old boundaries will dissolve. 'Either/or' limitations will be replaced by 'both/and' complementarity.

> *Religion without science is blind,*
> *Science without religion is lame.*
> *(Albert Einstein)*[34]

Politically, for example, we will surely transcend the old Left-Right divisions. The Left emphasises compassion and justice — but sometimes at the expense of disempowering people, of reinforcing a sense of victimhood; while the Right stresses individual power and responsibility, but often at the expense of our sense of connectedness. The Left disempowers, while the Right disconnects. The new politics needs to celebrate both our power and uniqueness *and* our love and Oneness.

Such transcendence of duality will reflect the re-emergence of the Goddess — of 'feminine' energy. In the Old Age, there has been an excess of masculine energy — leading to a world ruled by power, control, aggression, domina-

tion, exploitation, more-is-better, competition, fragmenta-
tion, categorisation, hierarchy and logic. Those who
embody such values — male and female — have become
selfish, competitive, materialistic, and cut off from their
own inner worlds.

In recent decades, however, there has been a rising
reverence for feminine energy — for cooperation, synthesis,
emotionality, intuition, empathy, responsiveness, imagination, ethics, faith, inspiration, spirituality — not as an
alternative to 'masculine' values, but as a crucial *balancing*
force. In the New Age, feminine energy will be valued as
highly as masculine energy. Both will be seen as essential
aspects of the whole balanced individual, and of a whole
balanced society.

The 'Old Age' has been dominated by the metaphor of
struggle and conflict. The planet has been seen as a hostile
environment, in which we must struggle to survive against
the brutal forces of Nature. We have stubbornly perceived
opposites: good and evil, friend and foe, subject and object,
alive and dead, light and dark, heaven and hell. Everything
is a battle. (Within the old world view, for example, peace
is — curiously — said to be achieved via massive spending on
lethal weapons.)

Darwin, Marx and Freud all saw progress arising at the
cost of conflict, suffering and even violent revolution. As
in Jane Fonda's concept of 'going for the burn', the idea is
that if it doesn't hurt, it isn't doing us any good. The Old
Age has nobilised struggle and hardship. We have become
addicted to suffering, believing it is the only path towards
growth.

The new metaphysics turns this approach on its head;
and here it departs radically from Eastern and Western
mysticism, which has too often promoted self-denial,

poverty and deprivation. The new spirituality suggests that we can grow through love, joy, abundance and laughter! We can grow by learning how to consciously create our own reality.

> *With all due respect, you created the idea that*
> *suffering could bring you Home. God created*
> *the idea that beauty, wonder, delight and peace*
> *could bring you Home.*
>
> *(Bartholomew)*[35]

A Course In Miracles reminds us that learning through rewards is far more effective and lasting than learning through punishment. We have been taught that it is somehow more spiritual to be miserable: 'But 'good' and 'deprivation' are opposites, and cannot meaningfully join in any way. It is like saying that the moon and sun are one because they come with night and day, and so they must be joined. Yet sight of one is but the sign that the other has disappeared from sight.'[36]

Seth, similarly, says there is no merit in self-sacrifice; indeed, that it usually means being a burden to others: 'Suffering is not good for the soul, unless it teaches you how to stop suffering. That is its purpose.'[37] Any suffering is caused by misdirected energy, which we must learn to use more positively. True spirituality, says Seth, 'rings and sings through the universe, and through your entire personality. It is a sense of joy that makes all creativity probable ...'[38] Nor do we need to have experienced misery in order to *appreciate* joy! As Lazaris points out, 'You didn't need to drink sour milk first to know that the sweet taste of ice-cream was delightful.'[39]

Many have suggested that the New Age will be marked

by the Second Coming of Christ. (Seth, for example, suggests that St. Paul will be born again, to correct the distorted remnants of Jesus' teachings and found a new Christianity.[40]) However, most sources concur that, although many great teachers will appear, the Second Coming is meant *symbolically* — an awakening of the 'Christ consciousness' within each of us: a spiritual renaissance; the coming of the new vision of reality; the transcendent moment-by-moment awareness that we are spiritual beings, that reality is an illusion we create, and that any limitations to our potential are all in the mind.

As we make this shift — not merely intellectually, but from a deep sense of inner knowing, of remembering — our consciousness takes a breathtaking quantum leap. We escape from the mundane wheel of life, and enter into the magic spiral. Then life can never be the same again.

The new vision reaches beyond the perennial philosophy in its practical and joyous spirituality, and stretches beyond the new science in its vision of consciousness and reality. It offers a transcendent way-of-seeing which restores our wholeness, our connectedness, our divinity, our power, our sense of meaning and purpose, our aliveness. It can take us, riding the crest of a tidal wave, into the future of our Dreams.

The New Age was not born in the 1960s; nor will it suddenly come into being in the year 2000. It begins in each of us when we awaken from our slumbers, when we step across the bridge of belief, when we discover for ourselves that the new metaphysics is not a crazy delusion, not idealistic fantasy, but a loving, expansive, spiritual approach to everyday life which really *works*, which delivers its promise. The New Age begins, for each of us, when we learn how to live magically.

The moon's the same old moon,
The flowers exactly as they were,
Yet I've become the thingness
Of all the things I see!

(Bunan)[41]

PART TWO
LIVING MAGICALLY

1

The Inner Journey

*You are a multidimensional personality, and
within you lies the knowledge about yourself,
your challenges and problems, that you will ever
need to know.*

(Seth)[1]

When the gods created heaven and earth — according to an
old Eastern story — they were left with just one problem:
where to hide Truth. They did not want it to be too
obvious, since observing the search would provide them
with great amusement. One god suggested placing it at the
top of the highest mountain; another on the farthest star.
A third god said it should be hidden in the deepest and
darkest abyss; and another suggested the dark side of the
moon. Finally, the oldest and wisest god said, 'No. We will
hide Truth inside the heart of each and every human being.
That way, they will search for it all over the universe before
discovering it.'[2]

Perhaps the greatest truth ever discovered is that we
create our own reality. It is a phrase which often brings a
gentle shiver of recognition — as though it is a truth we had
always known but had long forgotten; a truth concealed
within our own hearts. It is an idea whose time has come.

When I finally accepted that I create my own reality, I
was excited but *scared*. It felt like a huge responsibility.
There was no-one to blame any more. It changed my
approach to global issues, to politics, to feminism, to
psychology, to psychotherapy, to personal relationships —

everything was turned upside down. Every conversation, every event, took on fresh colour and significance. I knew that I must *live*, must *embody*, this way-of-seeing — not merely hold it as an interesting idea. I was living in two different realities. I had to spend a lot of time alone, just thinking.

I felt scared that I would be seen as crazy — that I might even go crazy: that I would begin to see little green men, jump off a tower in the belief I could fly, or just sit in a corner humming 'Om'. Or perhaps I would simply be unable to communicate with people who saw the world in the 'old' way.

Then I reminded myself that I create my own reality! I didn't need to go crazy. I didn't have to block communication. And when I came across people who told me I must be, at best, gullible to believe in metaphysics (and why didn't I rejoin their random, meaningless reality?), then I had *invited* them into my world. They were expressing the part of *me* that saw metaphysics as some weird science-fiction fantasy! And by mirroring my own hidden doubts and uncertainties, they would help me to clarify my ideas.

Gradually, I learnt to live more comfortably with a 'foot in both worlds', and to revel in my new way-of-being. My personal and spiritual growth expanded into every area of my life, twenty-four hours a day, seven days a week, as I came to live more consciously in each and every moment — knowing that I had created that moment, and that it was an opportunity to grow. And as I began to *live* meta-physically, rather than simply believing in it, my everyday life became more and more magical.

> *Big questions*
> *life questions*
> *have to be lived fully*
> *with your whole life*
> *Not just mentally*
> *on the back of an envelope.*
>
> *(Miller Mair)*[2]

At the entrance to the Mystery Temple at Delphi was the inscription: 'Know thyself and thou shalt know the universe.' Similarly, Tao Te Ching says 'It is wisdom to know others; it is enlightenment to know one's self.' Since ancient times, the wise ones have said that our greatest quest in life is self-knowledge. Mystics have always known that we create our own reality.

Our everyday reality is a grand illusion, a dream metaphor, which we are creating. By exploring and changing our *inner* world, we begin to transform our *outer* world. And we do not need to undergo years of psychoanalysis, or visit a hypnotist, or meditate for twelve hours a day, in order to seek self-knowledge. All of the beliefs and thoughts which create our reality are now accessible at a *conscious* level. If we are willing to embark on an inner journey, we can discover *all* of the beliefs, expectations and hidden agendas through which we create our own lives, and begin to create the future of our Dreams.

We can also tap into inner wisdom and guidance, and discover our higher purpose. We can learn how to maintain inner peace, joy and aliveness. We can move beyond our five senses, learning to sense subtle energies, to work on the 'inner planes', to communicate telepathically, to heal with light and colour, to travel to higher realms, to contact our Higher Self and guides, and expand our awareness of unseen dimensions. Just beyond our 'common sense' reality lies an unimaginable wealth of metaphysical (beyond-the-physical) realities. As Seth reminds us, 'Consciousness is far more mobile than you realize.'[4]

> *Our normal reality is like each of us living in a tiny, windowless cell in a house that contains a hundred thousand rooms and covers a thousand acres of land.*
>
> (*Michael J. Roads*)[5]

So — where do you begin? If you accept metaphysics — whether very tentatively, or from a deep sense of inner knowing — how can you use it to transform your everyday life? How can you translate theory into practice, and learn how to 'live magically'?

Part Two provides step-by-step guidance on how to apply metaphysics to your everyday life: how to process your beliefs and thoughts, how to use affirmations, how to programme your future, how to 'listen to the whispers' that can guide you, how to recognise your payoffs and hidden agendas, how to heal your inner child, how to handle your emotions, how to awaken to your higher purpose, and how to work with unseen friends. The exercises involve exploring your thoughts, feelings, beliefs, desires, imagery and expanded states of awareness, looking at everyday events from a metaphysical perspective, and taking practical steps to change your life.

Although the exercises are 'original' (unless otherwise stated), I take little credit for them. Like most therapists, I have been inspired by countless different sources — from metaphysics to Buddhism, from object relations theory to Jung, from Gestalt therapy to psychosynthesis, from mysticism to shamanism. Many of the exercises draw upon channelled tapes and metaphysical workshops; and several seemed to be 'dictated' to me from sources beyond my conscious mind (as were many other sections of the book).

QUALITY OF LIFE

Write down seven words which sum up *honestly* how your life feels *at the moment*, the qualities which your life expresses. (It is important to write them down, rather than merely think about them. The action of writing, or speaking, is a stimulus to change.) Choose carefully, crossing out some words and adding others until your list truly reflects your current life. For example:

Joyful, learning, laughing, understanding, dreaming, inspiring, releasing, deciding, changing, opening, loving, sensual, dramatic, scintillating, creative, expressive, exploring, learning, building, limiting, intense, comfortable, dull, stuck, dreary, routine, aimless, repetitive, chaotic, sad, lonely, resentful, anxious, guilt-ridden, cluttered, exhausting, hopeless, helpless, frustrating, rootless, disastrous, fearful, uneasy, drifting, argumentative, serious, ambitious, succeeding, opening, touching, listening, intimate, spiritual, peaceful, transforming, aware, stimulating, exciting, challenging, blossoming ...

Looking at your list, decide whether your life is just as you want it to be. You might want it to be different again in six months' time, or even next week — but do you *love* it as it is *right now*? Assuming there is room for improvement, that your life is

not yet 'heaven on earth', make a second list of seven
words in which you transform any words which feel
negative, or mildly positive, into what you *really*
want. (The new list might include some of the
original words.) For example:

List 1	List 2
routine	spontaneous
lonely	intimate
limiting	expanding
rigid	flowing
serious	light-hearted
exploring	exploring
sad	joyful

Gaze at your second list, and repeat the words to
yourself several times — out loud if possible. Try to
absorb the different 'energies' of that set of words.
How might your life be different if you expressed
these seven qualities?

Many exercises in Part Two involve guided imagery, or
visual meditation. These are a powerful way of 'talking'
with your subconscious, since it deals much more readily
with symbols and images than with words, and does not
distinguish between a 'real' experience and one which is
vividly imagined. Inner journeys also provide one way of
accessing our higher consciousness, and our unseen friends.

Guided imagery is much more effective if you first enter
a deeply relaxed state — an altered state of consciousness.
Simply sit in a chair, or lie down, and relax in whatever
way you choose. You might focus on each part of your body
in turn, relaxing from your feet up to your head. Or you

might repeat the word 're-lax' several times, then slowly count yourself down from 10 to 1. Or concentrate on your breathing for a few minutes, just feeling your stomach rising and falling but without trying to control the breathing in any way. Or imagine yourself in a peaceful place. When you feel ready, start the visualisation, involving as many of your senses as you can. At the end, you might slowly count yourself up from 1 to 5, suggesting to yourself that when you reach the number 5 you will be wide awake, feeling refreshed and at peace.

Some people 'sense' rather than visualise their meditations; others find that the images are faint and patchy. Trust that whatever happens is right *for you*, rather than wanting the experience to conform to your expectations. (The more you practise, the more 'real' the experiences tend to become, but they rarely seem as 'real' as our waking life.)

Meditating regularly is probably the simplest way of expanding your consciousness, finding inner peace, and tuning into your higher guidance. Meditation does not demand sitting cross-legged amidst candles and burning incense, muttering weird incantations. Sitting in an ordinary chair, or lying down, is fine. You might choose to repeat a chosen word or phrase, gently returning to it whenever your mind wanders; or concentrate on your breathing; or 'watch' your thoughts as they drift like clouds through your mind; or contemplate a theme; or embark on a visual-experiential journey to the inner realms. Some prefer to meditate through movement, such as dance or T'ai Chi. Many people enter a meditative state without even realising it — perhaps while listening to music, jogging, walking in nature, gardening or sitting quietly.

If you meditate for as little as 10-15 minutes each day, you will soon notice the difference it makes, and it will rapidly become a high priority in your life. Meditating two or three times a day, for 10-30 minutes each time, is perhaps ideal but it *must* be a pleasure, rather than a duty! (If you find yourself meditating for hours every day, perhaps you should ask whether you are avoiding other aspects of your life.)

If you ever feel 'spaced out' or 'floaty' after meditation, try stamping your feet on the ground, breathing out sharply three or four times, or doing anything physical; or close your eyes and picture roots emerging from the base of your spine, going deep into the earth. Avoid driving (or using a sharp knife!) for a few minutes, until you feel grounded again.

It is invaluable to make notes on your inner journeys, since it is easy to forget insights and action plans unless you write them down. Also, the process of writing often brings fresh insights to mind, and helps to ground them in your everyday life — as anyone who keeps a dream diary will know. Keeping a journal of meditations, insights, dreams, thoughts, feelings and significant experiences can be a vital step in our personal growth.

INNER LANDSCAPE

Relax deeply, then imagine you are in a landscape or townscape of some kind. Ask your subconscious to give you an image which reveals something about your view of the world. It might be a familiar, foreign, historical or imaginary place. Look around this place. What do you see? What do you hear? Are you alone? How do you feel in this place? Ask your subconscious any questions which occur to you, and let yourself hear, see or sense the answers. When you are ready, gently come back to the room and write down what the exercise revealed about your way-of-seeing the world.

(When I practised this meditation, while writing this chapter, I was surprised to find myself in a small, dusty American town in the days of the Western. It felt relaxed, comfortable, but very much a 'man's world'. People hung about talking and drinking. From time to time, horses and riders would canter past. Then I suddenly realised that it was a film set. The bar-room whose porch I was leaning on, while gazing at the street, was surrounded by cameras, lighting and film crew. I was one of the actresses. And I had a vague sense that someone was making a film of us making the film!)

> *There are as many ways to freedom as there are*
> *people, because each heart has its own journey,*
> *and each awareness has its own experience.*
> *Each of you knows exactly where you are trying*
> *to go.*
>
> *(Bartholomew)*[6]

The meditations and exercises in Part Two are simply possibilities to explore, not strait jackets. You don't need to follow the instructions rigidly. Be playful. Be inventive. Allow yourself to be surprised. If something unexpected happens during an inner journey — perhaps one of your guides will appear when you were expecting your inner child, or you find yourself in a cave rather than on a riverbank — go with your own experience. Trust that your inner self knows where to take you.

Similarly, trust your inner wisdom in deciding which tasks to tackle, and when. If you committed yourself to doing every exercise in Part Two in the order given, you would miss an opportunity to 'listen to the whispers' which guide you towards what *you* need, right now, as a unique individual. As you read, some exercises might inspire or excite you, while others leave you cold or unmoved. Follow your own energy, and do whatever attracts you — bearing in mind that an exercise might be helpful next week, or in six months' time, rather than now.

Listen to your heart, follow your own path — and have fun!

THE BUTTERFLY

Relax deeply, then imagine yourself curled up inside a dark cocoon, which envelops you so closely that you can barely breathe. How does it feel? (Safe? Constricting? Suffocating? Secure? Lonely? Dull? Scary?) When you feel a desire to break free, gently stretch out — feel the cocoon easily ripping open, letting in the sunlight. You emerge as a beautiful butterfly, with wings ready to unfurl.

When you are ready, stretch your wings and fly into the forest. Flutter here and there amongst the trees, sensing the life all around you — the plants, birds, animals and insects. Feel yourself as a part of this living forest. And now fly up above the forest, and take on a human form. Look down on the trees, lakes and mountains far below as you soar through the air .... When you are ready, fly towards a mountain peak, and land. Stand on top of this mountain, and shout out to the world below: 'I commit myself to my own growth.' 'I trust my inner wisdom and guidance.' 'I am breaking free from the past.' 'I am opening myself to new possibilities.' (Or whatever feels appropriate and right for you.) Then gently come back to the room.

2

Take One Cosmic Egg

*Once you understand the symbolic nature of
physical reality, then you will no longer feel
entrapped by it. You have formed the symbols,
and therefore you can change them.*

(Seth)[1]

Let's imagine two people, Joy and Gloom, who visit London
one weekend. The first visitor, Joy, experiences a wonderland of historical sites, museums, parks, theatres, shops
and entertainment — a city full of friendly, smiling and
colourful people. Gloom, on the other hand, sees a noisy,
grimy city with crowded underground stations, overpriced
restaurants, jostling strangers and mournful faces. They
visited the same city, perhaps the same places, and spent
the same amount of money — but Joy had a marvellous time,
while Gloom was thoroughly miserable from start to
finish. Why?

The secret lies in their belief systems. Joy holds the
following beliefs: 'Cities are exciting places to be.' 'People are
generally friendly and helpful.' 'Life is to be enjoyed to the
full.' Gloom, in contrast, believes: 'Cities are horrible places
to be.' 'People are usually unpleasant.' 'Life is a burden — but
we all have to struggle on.' No wonder they experienced a
different London. While standing in the same street, Joy
would notice the creative window displays and smiling
faces, hear the laughter and smell the roasting chestnuts on
the street corner; while Gloom would see the traffic, litter
and inflated prices, hear the honking horns and smell the

exhaust fumes. They live in different worlds.

However, it isn't just that their *perceptions* and *responses* are affected by their beliefs. Creating our own reality goes much deeper than that. We create every experience we have. We attract certain people and events *because* of our belief systems. Joy would be drawn towards the shops and restaurants which had friendly, helpful staff — while Gloom would bump into those who were stern and morose. Joy would happen across the unexpected delight of street theatre or a parade, while Gloom might attract muggers and crooked salespeople, or witness a street fight. Both would return home believing *they* were right: London really *is* a wonderful/terrible place! Our beliefs are not based upon our experiences, but vice versa. Our experiences are *created by* our beliefs.

Beliefs, attitudes, thoughts, feelings, choices and decisions are the raw ingredients of the broth we call 'life'. Some ingredients result in a delicious, mouth-watering soup, while others will produce foul-smelling, unpalatable dishwater. It's no good blaming the chef if our own broth tastes disgusting, or is simply bland and boring — because we not only chose the recipe, but stirred in each ingredient with our own hands!

DISCOVERING BELIEFS

The first step in learning how to live magically is examining our beliefs: the most crucial raw ingredients of our broth. Beliefs are a form of self-hypnosis. They are the guiding fictions which we repeat to ourselves so often, and with such conviction, that we forget that they are simply themes in a script we have written, and act as if they were true. 'Life is full of suffering', we might tell ourselves — and we see confirmation of our belief in every conversation with our problem-ridden friends, with every disaster-obsessed news report (which we compulsively listen to), and with every fresh trauma and misfortune that we attract into our own lives.

The task of the subconscious is to confirm that we are right. It does not care whether we programme it to create laughter and joy, or misery and failure. That is not its job. It simply ensures that our beliefs and expectations are fulfilled, that they are consistent with what we experience, that the outer world mirrors our inner world. If we have contradictory beliefs, it will reflect that in the reality it creates.

Cathy was a client in her early thirties, who was referred to me after her partner abruptly walked out on her. It had happened three times before, with different men, and Cathy had reached the conclusion that she was somehow *making* it happen. We began by exploring her beliefs about relationships with men, which came from two main sources. First of all, like most of us, she held beliefs based upon her parents' marriage. Cathy's mother had been a martyr to her gruff, domineering husband. She devoted her whole life to keeping the house clean and cooking his meals, while he vetoed any possibility of her developing hobbies, interests or friends of her own. She died of cancer at the age of 48, when her suppressed anger and resentment emerged as multiple tumours. It was a grim, lifeless household, and Cathy had decided early on that, for women, marriage meant no freedom, no identity and no fun. Moreover, men were selfish, cold-hearted and dull, and yet it seemed that, for some reason she couldn't quite fathom, a woman needed to have a man around.

Cathy's second source of beliefs about relationships was cultural: pop songs, magazines, TV and so on. These added to her confusion. On the one hand, the media screamed at her that romantic love was like an oasis in the desert; it would solve all her problems, and she would live happily ever after. On the other hand, it warned her to watch out: *love hurts*. The oasis is just a mirage. It might be thrilling at first, but it will probably end in pain and tears.

Since our beliefs create our experiences, Cathy's love life faithfully reflected her mixed-up beliefs. Men would be crazy about her at first, echoing her belief in the romantic ideal. Then they would gradually turn into her father, becoming more and more selfish and domineering, confirming her beliefs about what men were 'really' like. She, in turn, would become more and more pathetic and martyr-like, like her mother. Finally, the man would do what she both wished and feared her father would do: he would walk out. And she would be left with a bewildering mixture of emotions: shock, hurt, relief, resentment, confusion, anxiety, and a collapse of her fragile self-esteem.

As she gradually changed her beliefs, Cathy found that she was meeting different kinds of men. In the past, she had only come across the 'strong, silent men' who fitted her old script. But as she began to believe that men could be gentle, caring and sensitive, such men appeared as if by magic! Her reality began to confirm her new beliefs.

We all have certain 'core beliefs' which sum up our views of reality. We might believe that life is full of struggle and hardship, or that it is a delightful, challenging and exciting journey. We might believe that other people are selfish, greedy and unpleasant, or that folk are generally kind and loving. We might believe that people can never change, and there's no point in trying, or that life means forever growing and changing. We might believe we are helpless in the arms of fate/God/luck, or that we have control of our own destiny.

Whether or not we are aware of it, we *all* have beliefs about the nature of life, people, relationships, health, work, money, success, pleasure, the world and ourselves — and these beliefs form the basis of the reality we create. Whatever our beliefs, our subconscious mind will ensure that they are confirmed, over and over again, until we get the message: our beliefs create our experiences.

We all know intuitively that if someone firmly believes they are inadequate and worthless, that the world is a rotten place and that life is full of suffering, then they will not have a joyous, exuberant and loving life. It is so obvious that it sounds like 'common sense'. However, we make the mistake of assuming that beliefs *follow* experience—that we come to believe the world is a rotten place *because* we are treated badly. The reality, according to the new spirituality, is that our beliefs about the world *attract* experiences which confirm those beliefs. Like attracts like. The more intense the belief, the more magnetically we attract the corresponding experiences.

(I do not pretend to understand precisely how this occurs, just as I do not 'understand' why an apple falls to the ground. Scientists explain the descending apple by talking about 'the law of gravity'. I understand how beliefs create experiences in terms of 'the law of resonance', or 'law of manifestation' — that is, reality manifests according to our beliefs and expectations, since like attracts like. Neither law actually *explains* anything; they simply describe *what happens*.)

> *Whatever you send out is what you draw back*
> *in. Take responsibility for the thoughts and*
> *emotions you send out, for they go into the*
> *universe and create the events and circumstances*
> *that come back to you.*
>
> (Orin)[2]

Graham, 28, was quiet, self-effacing and likeable — but his life was a disaster zone. As soon as a new relationship or job came along, it began to grow sour. Everything in his life seemed to go wrong. Even his houseplants, he laughed, quickly withered and died!

When Graham was three years old, his father had deserted the family. His mother, preoccupied with paying the bills, seemed to have little time and energy for her children — particularly Graham who, as the only boy, was a bitter reminder of her husband. He recalled excitedly bringing home a drawing from school, which a teacher had praised. His mother glanced at it and grunted 'Is that the best you can manage?'; he later found the picture in the bin. He sobbed as he relived the painful memory.

Graham grew up believing 'I'm worthless', 'I'm a failure', 'Men are selfish and wicked', and 'No-one will ever love me.' As a result, despite his good looks and affable personality, women scarcely gave him a second glance. His longest relationship had lasted three months, and he had few friends. Men had beaten him up on several occasions, for no apparent reason. At work, he had been used and abused repeatedly, each time becoming so anxiety-ridden and exhausted that he had handed in his notice. His reality accurately reflected his belief system.

If we do indeed reap what we sow, then it seems sensible to take a careful look at our packet of seeds — particularly in those areas of our lives which go either particularly well or badly. From the effortless, smooth-running parts of our lives — perhaps friendships, marriage or career — we can learn *how to create success*. What kinds of beliefs and expectations underlie the successful parts of our lives? From the difficult aspects — perhaps family relationships, money or health — we find out what needs to change. Which beliefs are creating our problems in those areas?

These beliefs are not hidden and mysterious. They are what we are telling ourselves every hour of the day, year in and year out. We simply don't listen to ourselves! By learning to listen, by switching our attention to our *inner* world, we take the first steps towards creating joy and success in our lives.

When Alison first walked into my office, she confessed with a weak smile, 'Life seems to have it in for me!' She had revealed a core belief before even sitting down! She went on to catalogue a long history of disasters: from her mother dying when she was six years old, through to the latest traumas of seeing her cat killed by a car and being made redundant. Her ex-husband used to beat her up and she was the mother of a teenage child with a severe visual handicap. I had to interrupt her flow of catastrophes to suggest that we try to understand what was going on *beneath* the surface.

Alison's parents met as teenagers, at a drunken party which resulted in her mother's pregnancy. Due to family pressures her parents married, but they reminded Alison constantly that she was neither planned nor wanted. She was a sickly child, frequently in and out of hospital. After her mother died in a car crash she was sent to live with an aunt, who was barely more welcoming than her own parents had been. She grew up believing that she had no right to be alive, let alone deserved any happiness. If she had a brief glimpse of life's pleasures, then 'bad luck' would quickly follow. Her core beliefs were 'I have no right to be alive' and, with somewhat convoluted logic, 'I am being forced to stay alive as a punishment for being born.' (She had attempted suicide twice.)

The recurrent thoughts which ran through Alison's

mind, day after day, included 'What's going to go wrong today?', 'I'm sure it will be Renata (her daughter) next', 'Why can't I get anything right?' and 'No-one wants anything to do with me — and I'm not surprised.' She was so full of self-hatred that she made life into a torture chamber. Her world repeatedly 'proved' to her that she was wicked and worthless, and was being punished.

Gradually, Alison came to question her core beliefs and realised that, in a moment, she could move from despair to inner peace by being loving and forgiving towards herself. By catching herself saying 'You stupid woman, can't you even pour a cup of tea without spilling it?' and instead thinking, 'OK, Alison, you seem a bit shaky today. What's bothering you?', she discovered she wasn't so bad after all. She came to value what she had learnt from her difficult childhood, and to let go of the past. As she learnt to be a friend to herself, she attracted close friends for the first time — and the disasters which had become an accepted part of her life became more and more rare.

> *It is your belief system that runs every moment of your lives.*
>
> *(Bartholomew)*[3]

PROCESSING BELIEFS

Make a list of your beliefs about some or all of the following:
myself, the world, life, work, relationships, love, sex,

health, success, money, my career, my looks, parents, children, knowledge, responsibility, beliefs, the meaning of life, men, women, adulthood, religion, good and evil, reality, luck, change, death, pleasure, fun, limitations, creativity, my body, retirement, leisure.

Choose one of these topics, then scribble down everything that comes into your head about it. (Don't just *think* about it. With all of the exercises in this book, it's important to write down your ideas, or speak them into a tape recorder. The *action* of writing or speaking somehow opens us to change.) Don't censor certain thoughts — 'That's inconsistent' or 'I'm not sure that's relevant', or 'I don't want to believe that!' Just brainstorm as many ideas as possible, including ideas which seem to *you* like obvious truths. You might fill half a page or a dozen pages before you come to a standstill. Note any feelings that come up as you write. ('Felt upset as I wrote this one down.')

Then begin to sift through what you have written. What are your central beliefs and attitudes about this topic? Where have these beliefs come from? What contradictions emerge from what you have written? Do you hold other beliefs which might 'explain' the contradictions? (For example: 'Everyone is creative' and 'I'm not creative' might be bridged by the belief that 'I'm different from other people.') Make a summary list of your beliefs about this topic — including the contradictions.

Don't dismiss any of your beliefs by saying 'everyone believes that'. It is most unlikely that 'everyone' does — and in any case, if *you* believe it, then it is affecting

your life, so you need to examine it. We all surround
ourselves with people who share our beliefs so that
we feel comfortable, so it's often the 'obvious truths'
which we most need to question.

How are your beliefs reflected in your life? How
might they affect you in future? Would you like to
change any of these beliefs?

Repeat the exercise with other topics.

(*Note:* You might wish to use scrap paper for this
'processing' exercise, so that you can later throw
away or burn the negative thoughts and beliefs.)

Sally, like so many women, was full of negative beliefs
about her body and food. She constantly restrained her
eating for fear of putting on weight. She seriously believed
that she could gain three pounds by eating a cream cake
— and her body valiantly struggled to prove her right! She
looked on her body as an enemy, and groaned whenever
she looked in a mirror.

At first, Sally was somewhat bewildered by my suggestion that her body was just trying to confirm her beliefs and
that, if she honestly believed her body would maintain its
weight, regardless of what she ate, then it would do so.
Gradually, however, as she took responsibility for other
areas of her life, and began to feel empowered, she came
to like and trust her body — and it responded.

Most of us are labouring under beliefs which limit our
potential, or create personal trauma and suffering, or
which deprive us of the magic and joy of being alive. See
whether you recognise yourself in any of the following
limiting beliefs:

1.   Life is full of conflict and suffering.

2. It's a struggle to survive.
3. Happiness never lasts long.
4. People are basically selfish and greedy.
5. All men are...
6. All women are...
7. All children are...
8. Women have it really tough.
9. Men don't cry.
10. We only grow through pain and suffering.
11. I'm a hopeless failure.
12. The world is heading for disaster.
13. We live in a violent society.
14. Love hurts.
15. I'm a mess because of my childhood.
16. People become frail and sick as they get older.
17. There isn't enough to go round.
18. No-one really loves/understands me.
19. My health is never good.
20. Schooldays are the best days of your life.
21. Life is meaningless and futile.
22. It's wrong to get angry.
23. I've always been unlucky.
24. Self-denial is good for you.
25. Doctor knows best.
26. I'm too old to change.
27. I can't help how I feel.
28. I have to justify my existence.
29. The devil makes work for idle hands.
30. It's dangerous to walk the streets at night.
31. I can't help being ...
32. Life's miserable without a partner.
33. I'm always short of money.
34. Life is a rat race.

35. I don't deserve to be happy.
36. I never have enough time.
37. If only my husband/wife/parents/children would let me ...
38. Everyone gets ill from time to time.
39. You're over the hill once you're 20/30/40/50/60/70.
40. If only ...

You might wish to make a note of which limiting beliefs you identify with (and gradually add to your list as you process more of your own beliefs). Then consider what effect such beliefs might have as powerful, creative forces in your life. If someone holds the common belief that we only grow through pain and suffering, for example, then they are likely to create traumatic experiences at a fairly steady pace. Someone crashes into their car; soon after that the house is burgled; then a neighbour dies; then they discover dry rot in the living room — and so it goes on. They tell themselves they are just 'unlucky', without realising that they are the creative *source* of their bad luck. Thoughts are energy. Thoughts are magnets.

'Scarcity belief' — also known as 'poverty consciousness' — is another widespread belief system in our culture. It involves beliefs such as 'There isn't enough to go round', 'I never have enough money', 'Money doesn't grow on trees', 'You have to work hard for what you want', 'If I have more, others have less', 'Better save for a rainy day' and 'It's immoral to be rich when so many people are starving and homeless.' If any of these beliefs raise a martyr-like sigh, or an angry or self-righteous 'But that's *true!*' from you, then you're clinging to scarcity beliefs — and your life will reflect this. You will either struggle over money, never feeling you have 'enough', or you will be wealthy but afraid of spending it.

For centuries, material wealth and abundance has been seen as incompatible with spiritual growth. As Bartholomew puts it '... your minds have programmed you against wealth and pleasure, against things that make your eyes sparkle and your feet dance.' [4] We have believed that God wishes us to struggle along, barely able to pay our way, and certainly doesn't want us to have any *fun* with our money! Money is the root of all evil, dictates the puritanical thought of the Old Age. The New Consciousness suggests otherwise. It conjectures that God/dess, the Source, the Universe, the Force, the Light — or whatever term you wish to use — just might prefer us to enjoy life to the full, to open ourselves to the joy and abundance of the universe; that All That Is is perhaps a *loving* force, and does not want us to endure sorrow, poverty and hardship.

Letting go of our poverty consciousness will be one of the many delights of the New Age, and a crucial aspect of our spiritual growth. Instead of seeing money — or love, time, success or joy — as in short supply, we will come to see them as our natural birthright, letting them flow through our lives with great ease. Until now, we have divided the world's abundance into 'good' and 'bad' — it was OK to revel in the beauty of nature, but not to take pleasure in wealth. We could either be good and poor, or bad and rich: that was the choice. But as Lazaris reminds us, money (like nature) is just a set of vibrations, an illusion that we create — and we can have as much as we like of an illusion! There is plenty to go round.

This doesn't mean seeing wealth as our main goal in life, or as a guarantee of security and happiness; nor does it mean being wasteful and extravagant. It means learning how to create money easily and effortlessly, trusting that we will always have 'enough'. It also means *enjoying* it, using it, perhaps to create a pleasant environment in which to live, or to purchase experiences — whether travel, books, workshops, creative hobbies, social life, leisure or cultural pursuits — which will help us to grow.

If we hoard money, it soon learns that it is not needed, and we no longer attract it. We become a stagnant pond. By learning to be 'open channels' — spending money, giving it away, passing on old clothes, furniture and bric-a-brac we no longer use — we encourage more to flow into our lives. As we learn to take it more lightly, seeing it as a mere illusion, money begins to flow through us like a stream.

> *He who binds to himself a joy*
> *Does the winged life destroy,*
> *But he who kisses the joy as it flies*
> *Lives in eternity's sun rise.*
>
> (*William Blake*)

But what about all those poor, starving, homeless people? Lazaris uses the following analogy: Imagine that you hear a little voice squeaking for help. You move closer, and find that someone is at the bottom of a deep pit. What do you do? Jump in and keep them company? Or do you use your strength, resources and imagination to throw them a rope, so that they can climb out of the pit?

Many, many people — in Western society as well as in other parts of the world — are living in poverty. Unfortunately, limiting our own wealth does not help those people in the slightest. It merely adds to the deprivation in the world. But if we change our own scarcity belief, so that money flows more freely into our own lives, we have reduced — by one — the number of people in the world who struggle over money; and we might choose to use some of our wealth to help others — not out of guilt, but out of love.

Money always used to be a problem in my own life. I managed to stay out of debt, but only by being careful. For many years I huddled over a calor gas stove in the winter and ate beans on toast. If someone bought me an expensive perfumed soap, I would save it — not believing I would ever have another — until I found it years later, grubby and odourless! Even when I had money in the bank, I would buy cheap and cheerful clothes, books, food and other essentials — and save the rest for a rainy day which never came. It was never 'Jam today'. I never had a sense of abundance, of being able to splash out and enjoy myself. When I processed my attitudes towards money, the reasons became quite obvious. My beliefs about money were hopelessly muddled and contradictory.

On the one hand, I associated wealth with freedom, pleasure, joy, exuberance, travel and opportunities — and shortage of money with struggle, sacrifice, self-sabotage, fear, cold and hunger. However, I also linked wealth with being selfish, greedy, materialistic, hard-hearted, snobbish, and dull — as well as with childhood images from the Bible about camels and the eye of a needle! Poverty also brought up romantic visions of the struggling artist, fewer demands and expectations, and the kind of hard-headed practicality that was bred into me in the North of England. ('We'll manage somehow, so let's get on with it.') I also saw poor people as having more sense of community and warmth — as altogether nicer and more ideologically sound! What's more, I had memories from many other lifetimes of taking vows of poverty. No wonder I was struggling over money!

As I released my martyrhood and ambivalence over money, my old fears vanished into the air. Although my income was unchanged, money ceased to be a problem, a worry, a source of guilt and anxiety, and became a reliable friend. Despite minor lapses, I began to trust that whenever I wanted cash — whether to pay bills, attend workshops or take trips abroad — it would be available.

I came to see the world as an abundant and joyous place to be. I no longer linked money with struggling, coveting, fearing and grasping; instead, words such as bubbling, enjoying, giving, welcoming and channelling came to mind. My free associations about wealth changed dramatically: 'Prosperity flows through my heart as a channel of pure light — the Light of the universe, which offers to me its vast abundance. It is a key which opens doors to the wondrous possibilities in life. It is a stepping stone in my spiritual growth. Money is now coming into my life easily and joyously. The more I have, the more I can enjoy and share. I am opening myself as a channel to the Light.'

CRYSTAL CAVE

Picture yourself at the mouth of a cave. The cave is almost transparent, as though made of ice. It is a crystal cave. Feel your feet on the ground — then walk into the cave. It opens up into a fantastic cavern, which glistens and sparkles as though lit by an invisible Light. You gaze at it, stunned by its wonder and beauty. A tinkling music fills the cave, like wind-chimes. You walk deeper and deeper into the crystal cave, hearing your footsteps echo in the hollow cavern. Ahead, a brilliant white light is shining, at the opening to a passageway. You walk towards it, and enter the passageway — and find yourself in another crystalline cavern, dazzling in its magnificence.

In the centre of the cavern is a small crystal column, on which a golden chalice stands. The chalice glistens in the light. This is the Chalice of Abundance, placed there by your Higher Self. It is full to the brim of a wondrous liquid, which will bring abundance into your life. As you hold the Chalice, become aware of any resistance you might have to drinking from it. (What are your thoughts and feelings? What are your fears?) Then see your resistances become bubbles, which float away into the cavern, burst and are gone. When you are ready, drink from the Chalice. Drink and drink — for were you to drink a whole ocean, the Chalice would still be full to the brim.

If you have specific needs or desires, then throw a symbol into the chalice, and watch it multiply by the thousand, until it overflows the Chalice and floods out onto the floor of the cavern. If you desire more love in your life, throw a tiny heart into the chalice — and see the chalice become filled with tiny hearts, which pour out over the crystal column. If you want more success at work, toss a star into the chalice, and it will brim with tiny stars. If you want more money, toss in a gold coin, and you will quickly be ankle-deep in gold. (Note any fears or uneasiness you might feel as the Chalice gives you what you desire.) When you have finished, replace the Chalice — and thank your Higher Self for providing its abundance. Know that you can return to the Chalice at any time. Then gently come back to the room.

CHANGING BELIEFS

Let's suppose that, by now, you have become aware of one or more negative or limiting beliefs which you would like to change. (If not, just listen to your stream of thoughts or conversation for half an hour. Look out for any thoughts that involve 'if only', 'should', 'ought to', 'can't', 'but', 'trying to', 'difficult', 'limitation', blaming other people, feeling sorry for yourself, any fears or doubts, cynicism, guilt, judgements about yourself or others, feeling helpless, or beliefs in scarcity.) Now — how do you go about changing these beliefs?

1. Start by thinking about where a belief originally came from. Your father? Mother? Schoolteachers? Grandparents? Friends? Books you read? TV programmes? Your partner? Perhaps you cannot even remember. But the crucial step is to *take responsibility* for that belief. Accept that no-one forced you to believe it. *You* chose it. Don't blame yourself for that choice; you had reasons for adopting it at the time. Simply own it as yours.

2. Now choose your new belief — based upon love, trust, abundance, and the belief that we create our own reality. Here are a few examples:

Old	New
'Life is full of suffering.'	'Life is full of joy.'
'I never have enough money.'	'I always have enough money'
'Happiness never lasts.'	'Happiness always lasts.'
'I catch three colds every year.'	'I am always healthy.'
'I'm a failure.'	'I'm a success.'

'If I have more, others have less.'	'There's plenty to go round.'
'My childhood messed me up.'	'I learnt so much from my childhood.'
'I can't do it.'	'I can do *anything* I want to do.'

The new belief should be entirely positive. It's no good replacing the belief 'I'm a failure' with 'I'm not a failure'. If someone tells you not to think of a white bear, what happens? Right. It's like instructing a schoolchild not to giggle. Similarly, your subconscious cannot try not to be a failure without first of all picturing failure. So stick with success. Create positive images.

3. The next step is to work out why you are still holding on to your old belief. (This is explored in more depth in 'Cracks in the mirror'.) You can simply ask yourself this question, sit quietly with pen and paper at hand, and expect the answers to come to you. This simple method can work remarkably well. Or, if you want to have more fun ...

MEETING A BLOCKAGE

Relax deeply, then imagine yourself walking through a forest, feeling your feet on the ground, hearing the birds, smelling the flowers and trees. Walk until you find a clearing and wait there, reminding yourself of your new belief. Notice something coming out of the undergrowth towards you. It might be a person, child, animal, bird, goblin, or some creature you have never seen before. It has a scowl on its face.

You say 'Hello', and happily inform it of your new
belief: 'Life is full of joy.' The person or creature — one
of your sub-personalities — starts to argue with you,
telling you all the reasons why you are wrong, and
why you would do much better to believe that life is
full of suffering! ('You'll only be disappointed.' 'You'll
be left all alone if you have no problems!' 'You won't
be able to feel sorry for yourself again.' 'You won't be
able to blame your mother any more.' 'You'll be so
boring if you're happy!')

Each time it comes up with a reason, just smile
and lovingly tell it that you *now* wish to give up
your old payoffs, and believe that life is full of joy.
Hug the person or creature, give it your love, and
walk on along the forest back to the room, and
make notes on your resistance to change.

4.   Now, deal with your resistance. Decide whether you
will give up your old payoffs, such as blaming other people,
feeling sorry for yourself, or asking for love by creating
problems. Are you willing to take responsibility for your
life, to accept that we create our own reality? Are you
willing to be loving towards yourself and others, to seek
love by *being* love, rather than waiting for others to love
you first? Are you willing to let go of the past and reach
for the future? Take time to think about it.

Don't punish yourself for your old beliefs, or you merely
add paraffin to the fire. People never change for the better
by being hated, judged and condemned. We change by
being forgiven, loved and believed in. Learn to love and
forgive yourself.

5.   If you are ready and willing, change your old belief. For just 5-10 minutes each day, repeat the new belief to yourself, over and over again. Don't do it automatically, as though you were reciting a shopping list. Instead focus on it, think about it, feel it, desire it. Even better, write out your new belief, again and again, until it comes to feel a part of you — and note any thoughts or feelings which come up as you do so. During the rest of the day, try to catch yourself if you have any thoughts or emotions based on your old belief, and remind yourself of your new belief.

Also, write your new belief on small cards, which you can place on mirrors, doors, dressing table, fridge, the dashboard of your car, in your diary and so on, as repeated reminders. Or ask your inner wisdom for a symbol of this new belief, accept whatever image comes to mind, and draw this on the cards.

Positive thoughts and beliefs (or 'affirmations') and imagery can be used in every area of our lives. Let's suppose you have an important letter to write — perhaps an application for a job. You might find yourself procrastinating, because you see it as an enormous task which will take up all your time and energy for *weeks!*

Instead, try using affirmations and imagery. Tell yourself 'Writing this letter will be easy and fun' (not that it 'won't be difficult', or you still associate it with the word 'difficult'). Picture yourself posting the letter, and feeling that it *was* a simple matter after all! It is amazing what a difference these simple techniques can make.

Yesterday, I had to change a headlamp bulb on my car. I found myself mentally putting aside half the afternoon for the task as I struggled over the incomprehensible jargon in my handbook. Then I caught myself, and saw it as an opportunity to have fun and learn something new. I briefly imagined myself washing my hands after completing this simple task. After this, the job itself took ten minutes!

We can use affirmations to bring a positive, joyful attitude to life in general — either using them as needed during the day, or putting aside a few minutes every day to affirm our beliefs. At the moment, I start each day with this set of seven affirmations:

I open myself as a channel to the Light.
I trust in the power and magic of the universe.
I am attracting more and more love into my life.
I am attracting more and more joy into my life.
I am attracting more and more abundance into my life.
I am willing to let miracles happen.
I open myself as a channel to the Light.

The lessons of *A Course In Miracles* provide many wonderful affirmations such as — 'There is nothing to fear', 'I could see peace instead of this', 'All that I give is given to myself', 'All things I think I see reflect ideas', 'Let me be still and listen to the truth', 'Light and joy and peace abide in me', 'Today I will judge nothing that occurs', and 'The past is over. It can touch me not.'

Any phrase or sentence which makes you feel calm, loving, joyful and expansive is an affirmation. Here are some more possibilities:

Whatever happens, I have created it — and I can handle it.
I have complete faith and trust in the universe.
I am letting go of the past, and reaching for the future.
I am capable of everything I dream of doing.
There is no limit to my potential.
The world is full of love, joy and abundance.

I lovingly create my own reality.
I release myself from pain and struggle.
I am becoming more and more of who I can be.
I love and accept myself just as I am.
I am listening to the whispers.
I am radiant with love and joy.
I am going with the flow.
Today will be full of exciting opportunities.
I accept the power of this present moment.
I release myself from my old patterns.
I have plenty of time.
I welcome and accept all my emotions.
I am loving, powerful and creative.
I am attracting more and more ... into my life.
I am that I am.

Just one suggestion: be careful about the tenses you use. If you use the future tense — telling your subconscious 'I will soon be at peace with myself' — it will just sit back and wait. Tomorrow never comes! On the other hand, if you *only* use the present tense — 'I am now bursting with health', while you have raging 'flu — your subconscious might believe this is *your* idea of good health, and do nothing! Instead, try 'I am more and more at peace with myself', or 'I am healthy, and becoming more and more healthy'.

6.   Begin to act *as if* your new belief were true. If you believe that life is full of joy, then you feel happy and excited when the post arrives or the phone rings, rather than feeling fearful or gloomy. Imagine yourself in a beautiful garden, dancing across the lawns in sheer delight. If you believe in abundance, then enjoy spending your money (even on paying bills!). You could buy yourself a

small luxury each week as a symbolic message to your subconscious, so that it begins to attract money into your life. Begin to see yourself as someone with plenty of money to spare. Vividly picture going on a wonderful shopping spree, buying everything you have ever dreamt of, with great joy and exuberance. If you catch yourself worrying about money, then *welcome* the thought rather than fighting it, or getting angry with yourself. The thought has come to the surface in order to be released. So listen to it, send it your love — then use a positive affirmation.

When you change your old beliefs, you might find you have sudden impulses which are 'out of character'. Act on them! These are leading you towards your new reality. If you have an urge to go for a walk in the moonlight, do it! If you think of phoning an old friend, do it! If you want to buy a flamboyant pair of trousers, go ahead! If you ignore these new impulses, your subconscious will assume you were not really serious about changing, and will carry on as before.

7.   Use your reality as feedback. If you change your beliefs but your life stays the same and you *feel* the same, then you haven't really changed those beliefs, or perhaps more deeply rooted beliefs are blocking you. The outer world faithfully reflects our inner world. It is a feedback system which reliably informs us of our beliefs, attitudes, thoughts, feelings and expectations. Sometimes changing beliefs will bring spectacular results within days: you feel radiant with health, your boss offers you a promotion, you meet a new friend, you win some money, you feel a sense of inner peace — or whatever your new beliefs would attract into your life. Sometimes you have to be more patient and allow the universe to bring you joy and abundance in its

own way, and in its own time. But if you *honestly* change your beliefs, your reality will begin to confirm it. You will *feel* different, even if your life is 'objectively' still the same.

If you find yourself thinking, 'You can't change thoughts and beliefs *just like that*', then it might be wise to examine your attitudes and beliefs about change! Old Age thinking — along with most forms of psychotherapy — suggests that change is inevitably slow and painful, or even impossible. It views beliefs and attitudes as ten-ton blocks chained around our necks. It condemns us as lifelong victims of patterns set up in childhood, the unwilling prey of our devilish subconscious, the helpless captives of our 'character' or genetic make-up.

Transformation *can* occur overnight — if we allow it to be so. Metaphysics invites us to *revel* in the never-ending process of personal growth, to delight in the everchanging scenery of our lives, and to befriend rather than fear our subconscious mind. Seth suggests that our beliefs are like children's playing blocks, which can be moved around with ease:

'... all creativity and consciousness is born in the quality of play, as opposed to work.'[6] Personal growth is supposed to be fun!

3
Through the Looking Glass

Ever drifting down the stream —
Lingering in the golden gleam —
Life, what is it but a dream?

(Lewis Carroll)[1]

Jonathan Livingston Seagull, in Richard Bach's inspiring novel, is no ordinary seagull. Jonathan *loves* to fly. While other seagulls fly in order to catch food, he has higher aspirations. Despite the risks, Jonathan flies for the sheer joy of exploring his potential, of extending the boundaries of what it means to be a seagull. Cast out by his flock, who fail to persuade him that life is merely a question of survival, Jonathan continues to pursue excellence in flight, and eventually discovers the unlimited potential of being.

As children, we learn that we shouldn't daydream. We are told not to 'waste time' in our inner world when we should be paying attention to the Russian Revolution or the wildlife of Tasmania. When parents or teachers mock our desire to become a deep-sea diver, an opera singer or a portrait artist, and encourage us to have more 'sensible' ambitions — perhaps to become a nurse, bank clerk or accountant — we obediently wrap up our fantasies with a label which reads 'This is an impossible dream', and so fail to take any steps to make those dreams come true.

It is the child who refuses to abandon Dreams — who stubbornly persists in believing that he or she *will* explore the depths of the Amazon, or *will* become a film director — who becomes the adult who will achieve those ambitions.

Our daydreams help to build our future. Nothing is realised unless it is first dreamt of, and believed in. 'You get what you concentrate upon' says Seth.[2] 'There is no other main rule.'

Every day, we can either be driven by the past — repeating our customary patterns and habits, believing in old limitations — or we can be propelled by our future, by our Dreams, by what we are becoming. The carrot or the stick: which is it to be? We can plod our weary way through the days, sticking to a monotonous job and loveless relationships, watching TV every evening, filling our days with meaningless trivia — leading lives of 'quiet desperation' in Thoreau's words. Or we can decide that there must be more to being alive than this and, like Jonathan Livingston Seagull, become intrepid explorers of life's possibilities.

Relax — this doesn't mean we all have to make parachute jumps, battle with crocodiles or conquer the North face of the Eiger! But it does mean clarifying what we truly want out of life — defining the Dreams which make us tingle with aliveness — and making those dreams come true. Enthusiasm — which means 'the God within' (en theos) — is the spark that lights the candle which illuminates our path.

The Old Age religions teach that we should not have desires, that we should simply accept whatever happens as God's will. But this is just a way of avoiding responsibility for our lives. If we create our own reality, we create our own future. The future will not be as God/dess or fate decrees, but as we design it. The only choice is whether we do it *consciously* or not. We are not awarded extra Brownie points in heaven for living a life full of suffering, nor for one which is dull and dreary. We simply live the life that we are choosing, day by day, to create.

I am responsible for what I see.
I choose the feelings I experience, and
I decide upon the goal I would achieve.
And everything that seems to happen to me
I ask for, and receive as I have asked.

(*A Course In Miracles*)[3]

LIFE REVIEW

1) Make a list of any activities which make you buzz with energy, which absorb you so much that time dissolves, or which give you a sense of inner peace and satisfaction. What do you really enjoy? What makes your heart glow and your spirit dance? (A walk on the beach? Gardening? Reading a novel? Writing poetry? Listening to music? Chatting with friends? Sketching? Jogging? Making love? Travelling abroad? Charity work? Playing with children? Certain aspects of your job? Which *people* make you feel good?) Make sure the list is based upon how you feel now — not upon what you used to enjoy, or think you 'should' enjoy, or what other people like to do.

Next, make a second list of any activities (or people) which deaden and deplete you, which leave you feeling tired, bored or under stress.

Now assess how much of your life is devoted to each list. Does this reflect how 'alive' or 'dead' you feel? How might you begin to change the balance so that you feel more and more energised?

2) Review your life, and where it is going:-
* What are your secret ambitions (large and small)?
* What are your strengths, talents and abilities?
* What does, or would, give your life meaning and purpose?
* What personal qualities do you wish to develop?
* What is your ideal lifestyle?
* What do you wish to experience in life?
* What do you need — physically, emotionally, mentally and spiritually?
* Is your work (whether paid or unpaid) just a way of paying the rent, or is it important to you as a person?
* Are you learning and growing in your everyday life?
* Is your life challenging enough? Relaxing enough? Loving enough?
* If you knew you only had five years to live, what would you do?

Remind yourself that this is not a dress rehearsal for life. This is it! So it is worth regularly spending time on this exercise. Be careful to distinguish what *you* want from what your family, friends or partner think you should want. Bear in mind that we can keep changing our goals — but unless we have a destination in mind, we are unlikely to set off at all.

What you can do, or dream you can, begin it;
Boldness has genius, power and magic in it.
                                        (Goethe)[4]

Our impulses, desires and Dreams are fingers pointing at the moon. They reveal positive directions in which our lives might move, and move we always will, since *being* means *becoming*. Change is the very process of life. It is through change that we grow and discover ourselves, that we begin to actualise some of the myriad possibilities of our lives. We can either freely choose to change, and enjoy the new challenges, or we can resist change until life forces us to grow, through unwelcome problems and traumas. Growth through joy — or growth through suffering. The choice is ours.

As Bartholomew puts it 'The beauty and the power and the joy of life is not in *what* happens, it is in the motion, in the movement, in the constant changing of *all* that happens. Joy is in the incredible dance of life!'[5] He begs us to learn to enjoy the changing scenery, rather than clinging to the landscape that feels safe and familiar. We always know what the next step in our lives should be — which area of our lives needs to be resolved or changed — and we need to find the courage and self-love to start moving. If ever we wake up in the morning and feel that this is just 'another day to get through', then our life is painfully stuck — and it is fear and limiting beliefs which are keeping us stuck.

Every day, we make countless decisions — decisions based upon either clinging to the past or reaching for the future. At any time, we are *either* learning and developing or moving backwards. It is not possible to simply stagnate for a while; and it is our choices and decisions which largely determine whether we are growing. We can make fear choices, which lead us to cling to the past — 'I hate my job, but I won't find anything better, so I'd better stick to it' 'I always eat hamburger and chips on Thursdays', 'I'd like to know Chris better, but I'm sure s/he won't be interested in me' — or growth choices, in which we reach for the future

— 'I hate my job, so I'll start applying for others, even though it feels scary', 'Maybe I'll try spaghetti bolognese tonight', 'What have I got to lose? I'll give Chris a ring.' Growth choices usually involve some element of risk — trying a new sport or hobby, changing your job, starting or ending a relationship, making new friends, going abroad, redecorating, moving house, joining a campaign group, being more open about your feelings, changing your routine or behaving in a way which is 'out of character'. Growth choices mean being *flexible*.

A freshly bought loaf, still warm from the oven, smells and tastes delicious — but we would not expect it to taste good a week later. We throw out any stale crumbs for the birds, and yet we sometimes expect our lives to stay the same and always remain satisfying. 'I was happy with life last year, and nothing has changed — so why do I feel unsettled?' *Because* nothing has changed! The loaf is stale. It is time to buy a fresh loaf, or perhaps some rolls or croissants this time?

> *Ask, and it shall be given you; seek, and ye shall*
> *find; knock, and it shall be opened unto you;*
> *For every one that asketh receiveth; and he that*
> *seeketh findeth; and to him that knocketh it shall be*
> *opened.*
>
> (Matthew 7: 7-8.)

Let us suppose that you have at least a hazy image of your Dreams — your personal and global visions of how life might be. Perhaps you want closer friends? Or a more comfortable and spacious home? Or a loving, intimate relationship? Or to sort out your marital problems? Or to be healthier? Or to achieve a better balance between work, rest and play? Or a more fulfilling career? Or to develop your intuition? Or work on your physical fitness? Or abandon your poverty? Or to travel more? Or be more self-confident? Or find a creative outlet? Or set up a business? Or spend more time alone? Or perhaps you want to have more fun, and laugh more? Or simply to be your own best friend?

At a global level, do you Dream of a more peaceful world? Or an end to racial oppression? Creative solutions to our ecological problems? A world in which men and women have equal rights? An end to child abuse and slave labour? A world free from the threat of nuclear weapons? What vision of the future most inspires you?

Whatever your Dreams, the steps towards achieving them are the same. We can certainly take shortcuts if we wish, perhaps using creative visualisation on its own and sometimes with spectacular success. But here is a slow-but-sure formula for manifesting our Dreams. It always works.

1. Develop your Dreams

Whatever you desire, the first step towards creating this new reality is to clarify what you want:

'I want to find three new friends who share my interests.'
'I want to learn to play a mandolin.'
'I want to visit India and Thailand next year.'
'I want to help in the peace movement.'
'I want to live in a small village.'
'I want to double my salary within two years.'
'I want to build my own house.'
'I want to express my anger more openly.'
'I want to find a job that I really love.'

Write down all of your Dreams, including as much detail as possible.

2. Why do you want it?

How will this particular goal help you to become more of who you are? How will it change and expand your life? Write down all your reasons for desiring it. Might it have any hurtful or damaging effects? Would it be a substitute for *inner* changes you need to make?

Being honest about our motivation is crucial since, at this stage, we might discover that it is not our *own* Dream at all, or that our motivation is somewhat dubious: 'It will impress my friends', 'It will be one in the eye for my parents', 'It will ease my sense of guilt', 'It will make me feel more secure', 'It will give me power over other people', 'It will make me feel special', 'It's what my partner keeps suggesting I do', 'It's the opposite of what my partner suggests I do.' (According to *A Course In Miracles*, 'Any wish that stems from the ego is a wish for nothing, and to ask for it is not a request.'[8]) In that case, allow yourself to let go of that particular desire, and work towards another Dream. Or you might realise that you want extra money, say, in order to have more free time, or so that you can help a charity, or so that you can travel abroad. If so, programme for what you *really* want; it might arrive in an unexpected way.

3. Where are you going now?

Which of your 'probable futures' are you creating at the moment? What is likely to happen if you stay on your current path? If you work as a sales assistant, but dream of owning your own business, what are you doing about it? Are you saving up, reading about business management, surveying the market, giving yourself a deadline — or are you just wistfully dreaming over the cash register, with no intention of making your dream a reality? If you fantasise about a warm, loving relationship, are you making an effort to meet new people, learning from past mistakes, and *being* a warm, loving person towards yourself and others — or sitting indoors waiting for Mr or Ms Right to knock on your door bearing a glass slipper?

Be honest with yourself. Are you moving towards the future of your dreams? Do you feel excited by the future that is unfolding before you? Or are you marking time, hoping your fairy godmother will wave her magic wand? We create our own reality. We wave our own magic wands. If you do not change direction, where is your life heading? Towards being a prince(ss)? Or a pumpkin?

4. Examine your beliefs

If we desire something which opposes a current belief we set up an inner conflict — so look carefully at your beliefs in this area of your life. Which beliefs or attitudes might block or limit this particular dream?

If you want to have more fun, for example, do you also believe that work justifies your existence, or that fun-loving people waste time, or that it's 'better' to be serious and heavy-hearted? If you want good health, do you also believe that health is a matter of luck, or that you are a sickly person, or that the body is a machine? If you want a nuclear-free world, do you believe that the world's political leaders are crazy warmongers, or that humanity is out to destroy itself, or that the world is a dangerous and evil place? If so, you need to change those beliefs before moving on to the next step.

5. Deal with your blockages

Life is exactly as we have created it. We are the artists, and if our life is a dark, jagged abstract when we prefer Impressionist pastels which dance with light, we should ask ourselves why we painted it that way. What did we hope to learn? What do we gain from clinging to our rough abstract and refusing to start work on another canvas? What is keeping us stuck?

Many of us are afraid of success. Do you have secret fears about getting what you want? Or unrealistic expectations about what success will bring? (Do you fantasise that if you lost two stone, you would suddenly be happy, self-confident, popular and successful? Or do you realise you would just be the same person, two stone lighter?) What are the likely consequences of success? What are your 'payoffs' for failing?

Write down 'I really want..., but I'm afraid that if I get it ...' What dangers lurk in the shadows of your dream? What might you have to give up? Scribble down whatever comes into your mind. Don't censor any thoughts — write down *everything*. When you have finished, examine your fears.

When Susie first came to see me, she had had a string of unhappy love affairs. Her life felt empty and meaningless and she was taking anti-depressants. She was convinced that if only she could find 'a knight in shining armour', her life would be transformed. However, when she wrote down 'I'm afraid that if I find a man who loves me ...' one evening, she was amazed to find words spilling out on to the paper. She discovered that she was afraid of getting close, afraid of being betrayed, afraid of finding that a relationship did not solve all her problems, afraid of feeling trapped, afraid of 'disappearing' as a person, afraid of admitting that men were not all bad, afraid of losing her friends, afraid of having no more goals in life, afraid of giving up her unhappiness, afraid he might die, afraid of feeling dependent, afraid of sexual intimacy, afraid of letting go of the past, afraid that reality would not match up to the glorious fantasy .... Susie had not found a lasting relationship because (among other reasons) she was too scared. She was afraid of loving and being loved.

Many of us are afraid of failure too. We only learn and grow by trying out new experiences, new ways of being, by reaching for the future — yet many of us are terrified of getting it wrong. We would be amazed if a child decided that, since crawling was a perfectly good way of getting around, it wouldn't risk falling over by trying to walk. After all, it would be crippling its potential.

Fortunately, young children are almost free from fear. They pull themselves to their feet, stagger a step or two, tumble over and try again and again, until they can walk and run and skip and jump. They do not see falling over as 'failure'; it is simply part of the process of learning. When it comes to riding a bike, a child doesn't say, 'Well, I fell over a lot when I was learning to walk, so maybe I won't bother with a bike.' They look into the *future*, not the past, and see themselves cycling.

As adults, however, many of us cripple ourselves with fears of making mistakes, of making a wrong decision, of failing, of feeling embarrassed, of repeating the past. We might kid ourselves that life is perfectly OK as it is, so why risk trying something new? ('Why bother learning to drive? I've managed so far. I'd probably only fail the test anyway.') When someone points out that *other* people can do x, y and z, we reply 'Yes, but they're *different*!' We are butterflies thrashing about in our chrysalis, afraid to break free.

> *Angels fly because they take themselves lightly,*
> *(Alan Watts)*[6]

Another possible stumbling block is self-image. Some years ago, I helped a woman to stop smoking. Lisa had been smoking for twenty years and felt unable to stop for more than a day. In meditation, she met a cigarette in human form, to understand what functions smoking was serving for her. The cigarette turned out to be a dirty, slovenly, foul-mouthed creature and Lisa realised that she was projecting her own nasty bits on to it. (Other people project qualities they admire — such as ambition, sophistication or clarity of thought — onto their cigarettes.) As she re-owned these characteristics in herself, she gave up smoking with ease. However, three months later she relapsed. The reason, we found, was that she had not changed her self-image. Lisa still saw herself as a 'smoker' who was struggling to give up, rather than as a non-smoker' (who might occasionally have a cigarette). She was blocked by her self-image.

Lazaris warns that reality always *follows* image. Our self-image should be ever-changing, flexible, growing and expanding. Unless our self-image stays *ahead* of the reality we create, reality will 'snap back' in order to be consistent. If you create some spare cash but your self-image says that you are always short of money, there is a danger that you will create an unexpected and expensive event — a house repair, breakdown or bad debt — so that your self-image can be maintained. Whenever our reality changes for the better, in a way which takes us by surprise, we should get to work on our self-image fast!

SELF-IMAGE

Pick an area of life in which you wish to move forward — perhaps health, work, relationships, money or spirituality — and scribble down whatever comes to mind about your self-image in that area (e.g. 'Me and health'; 'Me and work'). When you have finished — it might take five minutes or five hours — look through your notes and pick out the central themes. Is there a single word which sums it all up (e.g. loser, spoiler, thinker, cynic, martyr, goodygoody, complainer, doormat, groveller)? What sort of reality would a person with this self-image create?

Now think about the reality that you want to create. What sort of self-image would you need to create to support this? Scribble down everything that comes to mind. Now pick on a word which describes your new self-image (e.g. winner, adventurer, sparkler, powerhouse, inventor, joybringer, enthusiast, philosopher). How would this person think, feel and behave? In meditation, picture yourself creating and handling situations which reflect your new self-image. Begin to see yourself in this new way.

6. Desire, imagine and expect

Most of the time we create our own reality quite automatically. We get what we expect from life, according to our desires, thoughts, beliefs, attitudes, choices and decisions. However, the new metaphysics suggests we can interrupt this automatic process. Instead of rerunning programmes set up in childhood, we can create new programmes, so that we learn how to *consciously* programme our own lives. (If the computer terminology makes you feel uncomfortable, remember that it is not suggested that we are computers. We are the *programmers*.)

Seth suggests that 'Mental images, accompanied by strong emotion, are blueprints ... upon which a corresponding physical object, or condition or event, will in your terms appear.[7] Other channelled sources — in common with the ancient magical traditions — confirm this theme again and again. Everyone is a magician. Whatever we imagine, expect and desire (or fear) will be 'magically' attracted into our lives.

This does work both ways. The subconscious does not distinguish between desires and fears, between dreams and nightmares. It simply works to fulfil our expectations. I knew a woman who was terrified that her house would burn down. It was the worst catastrophe she could imagine. She dwelt on this potential disaster so often, and with such emotion, that eventually a freak electrical fault did cause a fire. She then said she had somehow 'known' it would happen, that all her fears had been justified — instead of realising that her terror had pulled it into her life. Her fears were the cause, not the effect.

People who are scared of getting cancer, or being involved in a car crash, or having a handicapped child, should be wary; their fears and imagining are a magnet for such an event. They can become self-fulfilling prophecies. As Lazaris says '... just put out a thought, a fear, a doubt, a concern, a hope, a wish, a joy — it matters not whether it's positive or negative in your reality — it will manifest.'[8]

Every single thought manifests in *some* reality — perhaps in our future, or past, or in a simultaneous lifetime, or in another dimension of reality; but it *will* manifest. The more intense the emotion, the more vivid the imagination and the firmer the expectation, the more likely it is to happen now, in this reality, in this lifetime.

Creating our own reality, then, involves making *positive* use of our desire, imagination and expectancy. With these three tools, we can carve and chisel the future of our dreams. We can become *conscious* magicians.

> *Thoughts are things; imagination is experience.*
> *Accept this and the gateway to other worlds will*
> *slowly swing wide for you and each day will*
> *bring forth new wonders, so that you become*
> *once more as a child, absorbed and enchanted*
> *by all there is of which to learn.*
>
> *(Gildas)*[9]

Let's suppose you want to be offered a challenging new job. In order to 'programme' this, start by choosing a scene which represents this 'probable future'. Imagine yourself in the new office, or at the successful interview, or signing the contract — and see every detail as clearly as possible. Look around at the furniture, the colour of the walls, what you are wearing. Use as many senses as possible — sense your hands holding the letter, hear the clatter of the word processors, smell the coffee that is brewing ...

If your Dream is to live in a country cottage, then picture the cottage as vividly as you can. Perhaps imagine yourself in a cosy armchair, gazing into a log fire, stroking the cat on your lap and sipping a glass of dandelion wine. *Visualise* the scene, *feel* yourself in the chair, *sense* the cat's soft fur, *hear* the hissing and crackling of the fire, *smell* the woodsmoke, *taste* the wine ... Try out various images until you find one that feels right. Nothing comes into being without appearing, first of all, as an image in someone's conscious mind.

Now, for just a few minutes at a time, focus on this image — and stir in desire. Feel your desire for this Dream intensely, in every atom of your body — stopping just short of desperation. The more emotion you can muster, the more effective it will be. Whenever you have a few moments, just 'flash' this image inside your head, feeling your desire. *Expect* it to materialise. *Know* that your dream will come true. Whatever we honestly desire, imagine and expect — so long as it does not conflict with our thoughts, beliefs and attitudes — *will happen*. However, if you tell yourself 'This is silly — it can't possibly work', then naturally it won't work! Reality conforms to our beliefs.

Many people begin with simple programmes, such as manifesting a parking space when they need it. As you drive into town on a busy day, just remember the three key words — desire, imagination and expectancy. *Without* taking your eyes off the road, 'see' a parking space just where you want it, and *expect* it to be there. It will appear as if by magic! Once you know that you can manifest a parking space whenever you need it, you will be open to making the 'impossible' happen. As *A Course In Miracles* suggests, there is no order of difficulty in miracles; if you can programme a parking space, you can create whatever you Dream about.

There are countless different techniques for manifesting what we want, using the tools of desire, imagination and expectancy. Here are three simple but powerful techniques which Lazaris suggests[10]:

THE FUTURE LOOP

This involves three stages of visualisation. Firstly, picture a scenario which depicts your goal or Dream, using as many senses as possible. Secondly, pick out a memory from your *past*, perhaps from your childhood, which makes your Dream seem a logical progression from what has been. (For example, if you dream of having a novel published, remember yourself scribbling away as an adolescent, or having a poem published in the school magazine, or simply reading novels. If your Dream is to own your own business, then picture yourself playing with a toy sweetshop at the age of seven, or deciding *not* to be wage-slaves like your parents, or managing the household budget as an adult.) Finally, picture yourself in the future *beyond* your Dream. What will your future be like, say, six months or two years *after* you have achieved your goal? How will your Dream change your life in the future? Imagine it vividly.

STEP IN, STEP OUT TECHNIQUE

Picture the scene from outside your own body. Then step into your body and look back at the scene. Then step back out, then in — and so on until it feels complete. Always end *outside* your body.

33 SECOND TECHNIQUE

Choose a *simple* image which represents your Dream. Then visualise your Dream for *exactly* 33 seconds (for maximum effect) with all the joy, desire, bliss and thrill of anticipation that you can conjure up. Then let your mind go suddenly blank, or switch to another image. (It is easiest to time this by tape recording a guided meditation which includes the 33 second technique.)

CONE OF POWER

(Lazaris[11] describes this technique, but it is well-known within magical traditions.) It is on my *Evening Tape*.

Relax deeply, then imagine you are in a grassy clearing in a forest. See the tall trees, bracken and undergrowth which skirt the clearing. Hear the birdsong, and the trees rustling in the soft breeze. Reach down and touch the grass. Use all your senses to make the scene come alive.

You are now joined by *at least two* helpers. They might be sub-personalities, friends, family, guides, your Higher Self, or 'selves' you have been in other lifetimes. Allow them to be whoever they are, trusting the first images that come to mind.

Discuss with your helpers what you wish to programme for, listening for any comments or suggestions. Then join hands in a circle, feeling their hands in yours — and picture your Dream, in symbolic form, in the centre of your circle. Surround the object with a small cone of light. Now, along with your helpers, begin to raise that cone of light, little by little, by focusing upon it and feeling your desire. Watch the cone of power slowly growing until it is as tall as you.

Allow the energy to build and build, pouring your intense desire and imagination into the cone, knowing that your helpers are focusing too. The cone begins to vibrate, more and more — then it explodes into thousands of fragments of light, which fall gently around you. Celebrate your success, thank your helpers — and gently come back to the room.

7. Begin to live your Dream

Whatever you desire, start thinking and acting as though it were already true — in whatever small ways are possible. If you want to make a trip to China then, even while it seems an impossible dream, start planning that trip. Purchase a guidebook, and decide which areas to visit. Estimate how much it will all cost. Talk to people who have been to China, and make a note of their advice and recommendations. Start buying one or two items for the trip. See yourself as someone who will be going to China. Don't view it as a game you are playing. *Believe* totally that it will happen. Do not even entertain the possibility that it will not. Relax — and let it happen.

> *The right shot at the right moment does not come because you do not let go of yourself. You do not wait for fulfilment, but brace yourself for failure.*
>
> (*Zen In The Art Of Archery*)[12]

If you desire a loving, intimate relationship, ask yourself how you would think, feel and behave if you were in that relationship — and do it *now*. Make yourself a candlelit dinner for one. Go to the theatre alone. Walk along the beach at sunset. Buy yourself flowers. Wear sensual clothes. Be warm and loving towards other people. Act as if it were already true. If you want a new car, then cherish your beaten-up old Ford as if it were a gleaming red convertible. Polish it with care, and gaze at it with pleasure.

When we act as *if* we already have certain qualities, experiences, relationships, opportunities or material possessions, we exert a powerful magnetic attraction for what we want to come into our lives. The subconscious mind hates inconsistency, so if you begin to believe in abundance, and it sees you living in a tiny hovel with a leaking roof, it will start working overtime to correct the imbalance. This doesn't mean becoming psychotic. It doesn't mean pretending you cannot see the peeling wallpaper and moth-eaten curtains, and going wild with a credit card. It means firmly conveying the message that you no longer want to create this reality, that you *now* choose to attract abundance rather than poverty. Know that you are already rich.

A friend of mine, who was unemployed and in debt at the time, decided that he wished to attend a certain workshop in Hawaii. He used affirmations daily, and *knew* that he was going to be there. Just three days before the workshop, he spoke to a virtual stranger about his firm intention to be in Hawaii in three days' time, saying he had no idea how it would be made possible. The woman happened to be quite wealthy, cheerfully handed him a large cheque as a gift — and he flew to Hawaii. Believing in your Dreams is a powerful magnetic force!

We create our own reality. The world is just an illusion.

Anything is possible. Miracles can and do happen, if we are willing to stop struggling and *allow* them into our lives. Like the White Queen, we should perhaps make a habit of believing as many as six impossible things before breakfast!

> *Life is a gift, and it is yours to learn how to receive, not to earn.*
>
> (*Lazaris*)[13]

FLOWING WITH YOUR DREAM

Imagine yourself sitting on a grassy riverbank. Use all of your senses to make the scene come alive. Then allow your goal or Dream to take on a symbolic form, and appear on the grass in front of you. The country cottage might become a miniature replica of itself, or an ear of corn, or a vase which stood on the mantelpiece. Your new job might be symbolised by a contract wrapped in a red ribbon, or a tiny typewriter, or a bunch of office keys. Look down at the grass, and simply accept whatever symbol appears. Now pick up the symbol, and lovingly hold it against you — allowing it to dissolve into your heart.

Now walk towards the water's edge, and step into the river. Feel the water on your legs as you wade deeper and deeper. Then allow yourself to be carried gently downstream, going with the flow. The river joins another river, then another, and the current becomes stronger and stronger, carrying you powerfully and joyfully towards your Dream. Enjoy flowing with the river for as long as you wish — then gently come back to the room.

Programming always works. Always. As Lazaris puts it, we always get what we want — but not necessarily what we asked for. So if you programme for something which fails to materialise, then you should not blame or punish yourself, or decide it was not meant to be. You should simply sit down and work out *why*. Perhaps your current self-image is at odds with your Dream? Perhaps you have not processed all your negative thoughts and beliefs? Perhaps you believe that programming doesn't work? Or that you don't 'deserve' success, or should be happy with life as it is? Maybe you need to try a different visual image, or another technique? Perhaps you just have to be a little more patient? Perhaps — just perhaps — your Higher Self knows that realising this Dream would not be in your best interests right now? Or — as we shall see in the next chapter — perhaps you have payoffs and hidden agendas which are keeping you stuck?

Whatever the reasons, discovering why programming might have 'failed' — as well as why it has succeeded — is all part of the learning process. It is not success in itself that matters, so much as the process of *learning* how to create success, *learning* how to manifest our personal and global visions — learning how to live in a looking-glass world.

4
Cracks in the Mirror

This slowly drifting cloud is pitiful!
What dreamwalkers we all are!
Awakened, the one great truth:
Black rain on the temple roof.

(*Dogen Zenji*)[1]

There is a story of a king who dwelt in the dark and musty cellars of his magnificent palace. His servants and courtiers would bring him tales of the beautiful palace and grounds above, but he refused to listen to their mad ramblings. He was not foolish enough to be taken in by such tales! So, again and again, he declined even to take a look at what lay above the cellars and lived out his whole life in the semi-darkness.

Life, according to metaphysics, is exactly as we want it to be. Our Higher Self is eager to give us a life full of love, joy, success and abundance; but it will not do so until we say 'Yes', and we keep turning our backs on it. Day after day, we choose the dimly-lit cellars. Why do we do this? What sort of crazy person would *choose* to have a hard time? Why do we cling to unhappiness and misfortune? What is the poison ivy that so jealously guards our dark fortress?

We might kid ourselves that the world 'out there' creates our problems, but the truth is that the source of all our suffering is the Ego. The Ego is the limited, separated, illusory self which cannot see beyond the end of its own nose. The Ego is our internal saboteur, our own worst enemy, which confines us to the dark cellars of our mind.

It is the Ego which leads us to:

- worry about trivialities
- feel anxious and fearful
- feel despairing, helpless and hopeless
- feel resentful and guilty
- want approval and admiration
- take things personally
- criticise and judge others
- feel empty and dissatisfied
- swing from one mood to another
- feel hurried and 'driven'
- strive to be 'perfect'
- be concerned with outward appearances and worldly success
- focus exclusively on goals and results
- cling to the past
- be afraid of change
- worry about failure, humiliation and rejection
- compete rather than cooperate
- be manipulative
- harm and abuse others
- be rigid and inflexible
- be unable to live in the present moment
- become addicted to drugs or alcohol
- desperately seek love and security
- want to be 'special' to someone
- feel that life is futile and meaningless
- take ourselves *very* seriously
- wait for the world 'out there' to be OK in order to *feel* OK

> *The glass in which the ego seeks to see its face is*
> *dark indeed.*
>
> *(A Course In Miracles)*[2]

The Ego does have an essential function. It is Ego that, like a moving camera, shows us what is happening in the world. Without it, we would not have any conscious awareness. While we have a physical body, we must have an Ego. The problem is that it gets out of hand.

The Ego was designed as a mere postal service which delivers messages to our conscious mind. Instead we allow it to open our letters, read them *and* tell us how to reply. Not only that, but we let it choose which letters to show us! Lazaris[3] compares the situation to a file clerk who is suddenly promoted to managing director, without having a clue of how the business operates. In accord with the Peter Principle, we promote the Ego to its level of incompetence.

Our task is to understand our Ego, so that we can recognise its ranting and raving. It is a slippery customer and will disguise itself in various ways; we must see through its masks, for beyond the Ego lies our true unlimited Self.

Here are five telltale signs that the Ego is in command:

1. Feeling 'better than' or 'less than' others

The Ego *loves* making comparisons — and this can be useful. After all, we are only able to see a chair, so that we can sit down, by comparing the look of the chair with the 'look' of the space around it. (Or, in the dark, by comparing the feel of the chair with the 'feel' of air, or a nearby table.) The Ego needs to make comparisons, to fulfil its duty as a messenger.

Problems arise when the Ego not only makes comparisons, but makes value judgements. If someone believed that tables were *better* than chairs, we would think they were talking nonsense. But if they tell us it is 'better' to be tall, or British, or artistic, or shop at Harrods, we just might take them seriously — yet such ideas are just as meaningless. The Negative Ego is quite bemused by the concept of equality. It simply cannot grasp that we are all unique but equal. It is the ultimate snob. Everything has to be compared, and judged as either 'better than' or 'worse than' the alternatives.

The Ego wants us to develop talents and acquire knowledge, not for the sheer joy and challenge of playing the clarinet, reading Proust or rewiring the house, but so that we will be flattered and admired. The Ego wants a loving relationship with the sole aim of feeling 'special' to someone — not from a desire to *be* loving and to be truly intimate. The Ego does charitable work in order to pat itself on the back, and feel self-righteous — not from a sense of love and concern. The Ego cannot love; it is afraid of love. It is selfish and arrogant. It has delusions of grandeur. Its driving force is to feel better than other people, to be separate from others, to feel 'special'.

If you take up metaphysics, for example, Ego will delight in trying to convince you that this makes you 'better than' other people. After all, this is the *New* Spirituality; all the others are behind the times! With metaphysics, you can create miracles. Wonderful, says Ego! The Ego loves playing games — and spiritual games are as good as any other. As long as it makes you 'special', Ego will go along with it (and will ignore the fact that specialness and spirituality are quite incompatible). Ego relishes any notion that there is one 'true' religion, which you happen to belong to!

In reality, of course, nothing makes us better or worse than anyone else. We are all unique. We each have our own mixture of qualities, characteristics, abilities and short-comings — and if we judge others, we are judging ourselves. After all, the world is a mirror. If we totally loved ourselves, we would not feel the need to judge others.

However, this doesn't mean we should pretend to love everyone and everything, handing out pink roses to passers-by in a sentimental haze. Nor that we should not form opinions or make evaluations. On the contrary, it's part of our ever-changing uniqueness that we have our own opinions and beliefs, that we prefer certain sports, hobbles and interests, that we enjoy the company of some people and not others, that we like certain poets, novelists and playwrights and loathe others — and that is fine. It is when we use our uniqueness to feel 'better than' that we separate ourselves from others and thereby create misery and suffering.

On the other hand, putting ourselves down — feeling 'less than' — is just another way of expressing the Ego. 'Oh, I'm just a miserable earthworm! Don't bother with me!' 'I'm so dull and boring.' 'I'm utterly useless.' 'I'm just a nuisance.' 'Why would anyone want to spend time with me?' 'I'm just a neurotic mess.' Seeing ourselves as *less* important than anyone else, or less worthy or deserving than others, is just another form of arrogance, disguised as humility or neurosis. When we transcend the Ego, we know that we are all equal.

FEELING SPECIAL

1) Make a list of what you secretly think makes you 'better than' other people, or 'special' in any way. For example: being intelligent, stupid, wealthy, poor, male, female, young, old, attractive, ugly, successful, happily married, single, tolerant, strong, athletic, sensitive, kind-hearted, loving, creative, talented, spiritual, insightful, well-educated, healthy, having a chronic illness, belonging to a certain race or religion, being left-wing or right-wing, being ecologically aware, being involved in personal growth, working for charity, belonging to a certain profession, having a traumatic childhood .... Be honest with yourself, and list all of your 'better thans' and specialness'.

Now take a good look at these 'better thans', and see how ridiculous they are. Think them through. Remember that we create our own reality; we have each chosen to be exactly as we are, and for good reasons. (If you pride yourself on being intelligent, for example, bear in mind that someone else might have chosen to have a limited intellect in this life in order to learn from the experience, perhaps because they have over-valued intelligence in the past.)

Choose two or three 'better thans' which feel particularly powerful. Are they maintained by anger from the past, which you hold on to? How might you think or behave differently if you gave up these better thans? Try out this new way of being, next time you catch yourself using a 'better than'. How does it feel?

2) Repeat the above exercise with a list of what

makes you 'less than' others. What makes you a 'miserable earthworm' compared with other people? Recognise that this is a form of self-importance — that everyone is perfect just as they are.

2. Playing victim or martyr

'Victim' and 'martyr' are two of the most dangerous games that Ego can play. Both are games which can destroy our lives, unless we simply refuse to play them any more.

Annie was a classic example of a victim. She had been a battered baby, grew up in a succession of foster homes, and then married a man who regularly beat her up. When she was heavily pregnant with their third child, her husband threw her against a chest of drawers, then kicked her, and she was taken to hospital with three broken ribs. Amazingly, the baby survived. A social worker was called in and, with a lot of support, Annie moved to a women's refuge and then to a small flat.

Within months, she was in severe financial difficulties, and had become involved with another man who, according to her friends, had a history of being violent. 'I know I'm a fool,' she said, 'but I just can't seem to help myself!' She knew she was messing up her life, and carried on regardless. 'If only I'd had a stable childhood, maybe none of this would have happened ...' Meanwhile, countless helping professionals scurried around trying to help her, feeling more and more helpless themselves.

Like poor Annie, many people find that being in crisis is their only way of asking for love and concern. They are afraid that if life went well, if they were able to cope, everyone would desert them. If they weep and wail and gnash their teeth enough, their hope is that someone will rescue them, sort out all their problems, *love* them. Of course, Annie did not *want* to be beaten up, but she didn't feel that she *deserved* any better, so she attracted violent men into her reality.

'Victims' are magnets for disaster. 'Oh, I know I shouldn't feel sorry for myself, but it's all so *awful!*' is their constant refrain. Victims create trauma after trauma, then sit back while others try to help — and fail. They live in the past, believing that if only they had had loving parents, or if only little sister hadn't been born, or if only they hadn't married so-and-so, then everything would be fine. They express their anger by destroying their own lives and thereby hurting others, while seeming to be wide-eyed and innocent.

The bad news is that *everyone* plays victim at times. *Whenever* we blame luck, fate, circumstances, heredity, our childhood, society, the government, other people or God — for *anything* that happens in our lives — we are stuck in 'victim mentality', and so disempowering ourselves.

The payoffs for being a victim are simple: it allows us to avoid responsibility for our lives, to wallow in self-pity rather than taking care of ourselves, and to punish others. This does not mean that victims are *consciously* playing this game, but rather that they have *learnt* to live this way, not realising there is any better alternative.

When we come across a victim then, we should never attempt to solve their problems for them, since this only reinforces the idea that they are helpless victims of circumstance, with no strengths and resources of their own; it disempowers them still further. Nor should we *blame* them for their predicament. Instead we should provide them with the means of taking charge of their own lives; then — if and when they are ready — help them to understand their payoffs and hidden agendas, so that they can choose to stop playing this destructive game.

Martyrhood is rather more subtle and sophisticated and therefore even more life-threatening, because it can go unrecognised. Yet we all have a martyr within us. Lazaris suggests, that if we *ever* experience *any* of the following, then that is our martyr, slinking out from its hideyhole:

1.   Feeling misunderstood.
2.   Feeling unappreciated.
3.   Feeling hopeless.
4.   Feeling burdened with unbelievable demands.
5.   Feeling saddled with insoluble problems.
6.   Feeling innocent of all responsibility.
7.   Feeling judged and treated wrongly.

'But I really *am* unappreciated!' Perhaps so, and *you* created that reality. Why did you do that?

During the decade I worked in the National Health Service, I saw countless martyrs — and a good proportion of them were the staff. Conversations in staff rooms frequently centred around the pressures of waiting lists, the burden of heavy caseloads, the 'hopeless cases', the lack of appreciation from management, the absence of support and the inevitability of working countless hours of unpaid overtime, at the expense of our personal lives. 'Poor, wonderful us!' was the unspoken consensus. Staff meetings reverberated with heavy sighs (martyrs are very fond of sighing) — and we were trying to help our clients sort out *their* lives! Not surprisingly, we rarely identified our clients as being martyrs. It would have been rather too close to home.

Martyrs seldom complain openly about their lot. They usually deny feeling sorry for themselves — 'No, everything's fine!' — but they make it clear that life is tough for them. They feel weighed down with responsibilities, but rarely accept any help. ('I'll just struggle along on my own.') They associate suffering with saintliness. Whereas victims live in the past, martyrs live in the future: a golden age when their burdens will be lifted, their efforts will be recognised, and they will be fully vindicated. But somehow that future never arrives.

While writing this book, I slipped back into my martyr for a couple of weeks. I found myself working twelve to fourteen hours a day, barely coming up for air, and looking forward to *finishing* the book so that life could begin again — rather than enjoying the day-by-day *process* of writing, and living life to the full. My external world began to reflect that all was not well. My garden wall collapsed in a storm; a tyre was slashed on my car and I received several 'wrong number' phone calls. I struggled for some time to understand the metaphors until an inner voice said to me during meditation: 'You're in martyr over this book.' Suddenly, it all made sense! I looked at my beliefs and payoffs, reorganised my writing schedule, arranged several outings — and felt an enormous sense of relief.

Lazaris describes martyrhood as 'silent and righteous anger that seeks silent and righteous revenge'.[5] Martyrs, he suggests, are out to punish. They are convinced that they are the only ones who suffer, and refuse to see the impact they have on others. Martyrs are never in the wrong. They always justify and rationalise their own behaviour. It is always other people who are at fault. They simply feel misunderstood and unappreciated.

As parents, martyrs teach their children how to play the game. ('Look at all I've done for you, and this is how you behave!' 'No, you go out and have fun with your father. I'll just stay in and scrub the kitchen floor, wash your clothes and make your dinner.') Children of well-developed martyrs learn that it is wrong to enjoy life, wrong to fulfil your own needs, wrong to express anger directly and that 'love' means self-sacrifice. Unless they see through the game, such children grow up to be victims and martyrs themselves. Martyrs breed martyrs.

Jessica was the daughter of a martyr and had learnt the game well. At the age of 17, she became pregnant to an older man who immediately deserted her. She was rejected by her family and moved to another town, where she struggled to bring up her son alone and unsupported. When her son was badly injured in a road accident, she nursed him to the point of exhaustion, refusing outside help, and comforted herself with the thought that if only her family knew what she was going through, they would rush to her rescue.

She became involved with a married man, who eventually ended the affair — but ten years later, Jessica was still convinced that, one day, he would realise that he loved her, arrive at her door with a ring and they would live happily ever after. In fact, her wardrobe was stuffed with new clothes, shoes, perfume and cosmetics which she was 'saving' for this fantasised future. In the meantime, she wore the same old rags week after week, lived in poverty and was 'faithful' to her ex-lover.

I had been seeing Jessica for twelve months before she admitted to herself that her lover would never come back. It was even longer before she realised that she wasn't sure she had ever *wanted* him to. It took a great deal of courage — and self-love — to admit that all her suffering had been in vain.

Unfortunately, Christianity has been built upon a classic

image of martyrhood: Christ on the cross. Suffer and get your reward in heaven! Ego is the self-righteous martyr inside each of us. It is the devil within; and if we recognise martyrhood in friends, relatives and colleagues, then we should remember: the world is our mirror!

MARTYRHOOD

1) Consider the seven signs of martyrhood listed above, and remember when you have experienced those thoughts and feelings. How did you behave in those situations? Who were you angry with? Who were you trying to punish? (It might be someone who wasn't even there, such as a Parent inside your head.)

2) Write down your payoffs for being a martyr. Why do you play such a destructive game? Do you enjoy feeling sorry for yourself? Does it make you feel special, or 'one-up' on others? Do you imagine you'll somehow be rewarded for being a martyr? Is it your way of being 'powerful'? Is it your only way of expressing anger? Who do you feel unable to forgive? Do you believe that life is full of suffering? Or that it is saintly to suffer? Are you reluctant to accept help from others, because you hate feeling dependent or grateful? Is it a way of avoiding responsibility for your life? Do you cling to problems because you do not know what else to think about, and what else to discuss with friends? (It is not enough to say that you learnt martyrhood from your parents. You *chose* to play the same game. Why?)

3) Now write down the *costs* of being a martyr.

What is the price you pay? How might life be different if you gave up playing this game? How would you then feel about yourself? Imagine yourself undergoing a sudden transformation, in which the martyr is forever banished from your life. How does the 'new you' behave, think, feel, talk? How does the change affect your personal relationships, work, finances, leisure and health?

4) Finally, make the decision: are you prepared to give up your payoffs in favour of the benefits of losing your martyr? If so, begin to *be* that new person from now on. Whenever you can, catch yourself before you play martyr — and instead be loving, forgiving, honest, grateful, responsible, hopeful, courageous.

3. Denying responsibility

Ego is desperate to deny and avoid responsibility. Whatever goes wrong in our lives, it will point the finger at others — our parents, our boss, our partner or ex-partner, our children, God, fate, the government .... It is always someone else's fault. If someone is angry with you, Ego says they're bad-tempered and unreasonable. If you fail to get a report in on time, Ego protests it was too tough a deadline. If a worn tyre bursts, it's the manufacturer's fault. The buck never stops with Ego!

The Ego is an expert at being defensive, at rationalising and justifying its own behaviour, at seeing itself as the hapless victim of a cruel, harsh world. 'Poor me!' is one of its stock phrases. Ego takes great pleasure in wallowing in self-pity, and defending itself against all charges, whatever the cost to others. It is dishonest and manipulative.

Blaming others or opting out of responsibility is a reliable sign that Ego is in control. 'Look what they did to me!' 'It isn't my problem.' 'I was nowhere near it!' 'I was just following orders.' 'It's the government's fault.' 'Nothing to do with me.' 'Men/women are all the same!' 'S/he made me do it!' 'I can't do it because of him/her.' 'This is all your fault.' Or, in a more patronising manner, 'Yes, I accept that you see it as my doing.' (Or, even worse 'Yes, I know I'm hurting you — but *you're* creating it!')

Since we create our own reality, blaming others is nonsensical. What's more, it disempowers us. While we believe that a problem is all someone else's fault, we are powerless to resolve it, since we cannot change other people; we can only change ourselves. Why give our power away to others?

The more responsibility we take for our lives, the more power we have to create life exactly as we want it to be. Responsibility is not about duty or guilt. It is *response-ability*: the ability to act.

> *The greatest freedom is to be responsible.*
>
> *(Lazaris)[6]*

Taking responsibility does not mean blaming oneself. 'Oh, stupid, terrible me! I created having a car crash last week!' This is just giving in to your Ego, which loves to play 'Ain't I awful!' If you have a car crash, then yes, you did create or allow it, but don't blame and harass yourself for that. Accept it. Try to understand why you might have chosen to do that. Learn from it, and forgive yourself. Don't pretend it was all the other driver's fault, even if they *did* crash into the back of you, or were driving recklessly. From an insurance point of view, maybe they were 'responsible'

— and they must deal with that. But once your anger has subsided, realise that you *allowed* the crash to happen. You attracted it into your reality. In a loving way, ask yourself why you did that? What negative beliefs did it reinforce? What are your payoffs? *There is no blame—just responsibility*. As we accept more responsibility, so we empower and enrich our lives.

TAKING RESPONSIBILITY

1) Think about times when you have blamed others, or refused to take responsibility for your life. Are there any areas of life in which you consistently deny responsibility? Looking back, what might you have learnt if you had explored your own role in creating those situations? Might other problems have been prevented?

2) Consider the successes you have had in your life. (All too often, we take responsibility for failure, but not for success. 'Oh, I was just lucky.') What has worked out well for you? What have you achieved?

Now look at how you *created* those successes. What were your positive beliefs and attitudes? Thinking back, did you use desire, imagination and expectancy? *How* did you succeed? What can you learn from those successes?

3) Over the next few days, practise taking responsibility for *everything* that happens. (Express your feelings at the time, *then* accept that you created that reality.) How does it feel to be more responsible?

---

4. Being busy-busy

The Ego loves to clutter up our lives with meaningless tasks, clutter and trivia, so that we're 'too busy' to grow and change. It convinces us that it is essential to read a daily newspaper, to watch TV, to mow the lawn, to iron the sheets, to read the junk mail, to darn our socks — just in case we decide to do something creative, challenging, productive, intimate or enjoyable instead.

The Ego is constantly chattering about its fears, worries and doubts, cluttering up our head with thoughts that go nowhere — just in case we decide to think for ourselves, to question, to explore new possibilities, to feel our suppressed emotions, to reach beyond our old ways of being, to develop a new vision.

Whenever you find yourself being busy-busy yet getting nowhere, you can be sure that your 'clutterbug' has taken control and that you are running away from change.

> *You don't take a monkey and make it into a*
> *mountain. A monkey is a monkey and will move*
> *from tree to tree. A mountain is a mountain and*
> *will maintain itself as mountain. Your ego is the*
> *monkey, your Self is the mountain .... You can*
> *choose to use monkey mind or feel mountain.*
> (Bartholomew)[7]

THE CLUTTERBUG

How does 'the clutterbug' express itself in your life? 'What is the clutter and trivia which absorbs your precious time? How could you simplify your life, to create time and space for what really matters to

you? What could you stop doing, or devote less time
to, or ask someone else to do? Imagine that you are
expanding, and seeing your life from a higher perspective. Where do you *really* wish to focus your
time and energy? Keep asking yourself throughout
the day 'Is this the best use of my time?'

5. Flirting with disaster

The Ego adores melodrama. It enjoys nothing more than
people's lives being destroyed — including our own. Its
greatest enemy is inner peace. Whatever we most fear in
life is exactly what our Ego would like to create for us. It
wants us to live out that gruesome fantasy, to find out
whether we could handle it. We fear that disaster *because*
part of us is hell-bent on making it happen!

Lazaris suggests that whatever we most pride in
ourselves gives a clue to our Ego's fantasies. (Look back at
your list of 'better thans.') One of my 'better thans' is being
very efficient and well-organised — my rising sign is Virgo
— and I have been known to smile smugly when others
display their lack of organisation, slowness or an inability
to spell. However, my corresponding Ego fantasy is of
losing my wits to such an extent that I am unable to work;
I am living in a filthy bedsit and the floor is strewn with
pieces of paper that I am unable to make sense of, final
demands which have not been paid, dirty clothes, plants
which have fallen over, unwashed plates and mugs — and I
am curled up in a foetal ball, wishing the world would go
away! (And my payoffs? Self-pity, and an escape from
responsibility.)

Have you ever secretly flirted with the idea that it might
be rather glamorous or exciting to be widowed young, to

go blind, to have cancer or AIDS, to go bankrupt, to be burgled, to be a social outcast, to go crazy, to become homeless, to be a drug addict, even to commit suicide ...? If so, beware! You are being seduced by your Ego's love of melodrama and, since it can feel thrilling to dice with death, you might be tempted to walk rather too close to the edge of the cliff.

Jack came from a family which was riddled with alcohol abuse. Both parents, his brother, and several other relatives drank very heavily, and an uncle had died from liver cirrhosis. Jack had always been teetotal, since he was convinced that if he ever touched alcohol, he would become dependent. Yet one day, in his early forties, he purchased a large bottle of vodka — in order to prove, he lied to himself, that he was able to resist 'the demon drink'. He was teetering on the edge of the cliff.

FLIRTING WITH DISASTER

What are your Ego's most destructive fantasies? Start from your list of 'better thans', and work out what the opposite extreme would look like. Or think about any fantasy of disaster which has repeatedly flitted across your mind over the years. Write it out in detail. Visualise it. Immerse yourself in it. Feel the fear, as you realise that your Ego actually *wants* this to happen! What would your 'payoffs' be if it came true? (Don't worry that visualising the scene might make it materialise. It is *suppressing* such fears which make them more powerful.)

Now decide whether or not you want to move towards that 'probable future'. If not, then put a large

| red cross through the notes you have written. Tear
the paper into bits, and flush it down the toilet. |

The Ego, then, has a whole array of negative beliefs,
payoffs and hidden agendas which limit or even wreck our
lives, and block our attempts to programme what we want.
It glorifies in struggle, self-pity, self-importance, self-
righteousness, self-sacrifice, punishing others, avoiding
and denying responsibility, dishonesty and manipulation.
It is afraid of intimacy, afraid of happiness, afraid of having
to feel gratitude. It fills our lives with trivia and clutter. It
makes us feel guilty, resentful and anxious, and encourages
us to cling to the past.

Each of us has our own favourite payoffs, the golden
oldies that we return to again and again such as 'When in
doubt, just feel sorry for yourself.' Which of the payoffs,
games and hidden agendas above feel uncomfortably
familiar to you? Which make you cringe slightly, or shift
about in your seat? Which make you think 'No, that couldn't
be me. Could it ...?' If you are honest with yourself, you will
know.

BEYOND EGO

Relax deeply, and imagine yourself walking through
a beautiful forest. Feel your feet on the ground. See
the sunlight dappling through the trees. Hear the
birdsong and the crackle of twigs underfoot. Touch
a fallen trunk, or the ferns at your feet. Smell the
rich, damp forest air. Follow the path as it winds its
way through the forest.

Then something emerges from behind a tree

ahead. It is one of your payoffs or blockages. (Perhaps self-pity, or specialness, or scarcity belief, or blame.) See what form it takes — perhaps an animal, a mythical creature, a fictional character, a younger version of yourself, or someone you know. Allow yourself to see it clearly.

The person or creature is blocking your path, so walk up and speak with it. *Assume that it has been trying to help you,* in some misguided way. Ask what it is trying to do for you, so that you can understand and forgive. Assure it that you now have other ways of handling life, or new beliefs, that it can now help you in some other way. Give it a new vision of your future, and ask it to join you. Then allow yourself to merge with this aspect of yourself. (Repeat as often as you wish, with other inner blockages.)

Then stride joyfully along the path, until you come across a waterfall in the depths of the forest. Take off your clothes, and stand beneath the waterfall. Allow it to wash away the last traces of your old payoff or negative belief. Then gently come back to the room.

Who is the third who walks always beside you?
When I count, there are only you and I together
But when I look ahead up the white road
There is always another one walking beside you
Gliding wrapt in a brown mantle, hooded
I do not know whether a man or a woman
— But who is that on the other side of you?

(T S. Eliot)[8]

In case we become aware of its tricks, the Ego tries to throw us off the scent, by projecting aspects of itself onto the outside world. As Lazaris humorously puts it, the Ego is not very smart, but it's smarter than we are! While Ego is playing its 'better than' games, for example, we will see our own worst qualities outside ourselves, in other people. When it chooses 'less than' games, we will project our good qualities on to others.

The world is a mirror. If we look around at our friends, partner, family, colleagues and acquaintances, we see our own reflection. 'Richard is so arrogant.' 'Mary has her head in the clouds.' 'John is very kind-hearted.' 'Julia thrives on having problems.' 'Tony can only think about himself.' All of these comments might be qualities which we refuse to see in ourselves, and could guide us along the path towards self-discovery. 'But Richard really *is* arrogant!' Well, yes, he might be. But why do you choose to comment on it, even to yourself? Why have you attracted him into your reality? Whatever we most dislike or fear in others is sure to be an unacknowledged aspect of ourselves. What we see others grappling with reflects our own struggle.

Of course, this doesn't mean that if a man exposes himself to you, you must be repressing that urge within yourself. But it will reflect *some* aspect of you. Perhaps your judgements and 'better thans' about people who do such things? Or your negative beliefs about men? Or maybe you have a desire to 'expose' yourself in some way — perhaps as an artist or politician — but are blocking yourself through fear of humiliation or rejection? If the 'mirror' is not a simple reflection, it will be a dream-like metaphor.

THE MIRROR

1) Think about the comments you make about people you know — both people you particularly like, and those who cause you stress and heartache. What qualities do you most like and dislike in other people? If you are honest, can you see those qualities — good and bad — as aspects of yourself? (If not, how might they be mirroring your beliefs?) What do you see others struggling with?

2) If you are having difficulties with someone, assume that the other person is an aspect of yourself which needs to be integrated, and try the Gestalt 'empty chair' technique. Sit in a chair, and face another chair. Imagine that the other person is sitting in the other chair — and start telling them why you find them so troublesome. Then move to the other chair and answer back, as the other person. Then back again, replying to him or her. Back to the other chair, and so on — moving every time you pause for thought. Continue until there has been some resolution of the inner conflict.

Jung termed these disowned aspects of ourselves 'the Shadow', and warned that they can become a destructive influence on our lives, unless we shine a light on them. The Shadow is dark, brooding Heathcliff to Catherine. It is the evil Mr Hyde to Dr Jekyll. It can lead us to our own downfall.

As Jung pointed out, it is necessary for us to have a Shadow, since we cannot be everything that it would be possible for us to be. We must choose which aspects of ourself to express to the world. However, if we kid ourselves that we are all sweetness and light, then our angry and hateful Shadow will manifest itself elsewhere — in other people, in our view of the world, in our body, and in dreams (perhaps as a dark, shadowy figure, or a thoroughly unpleasant character). Our Shadow will repeatedly taunt us: 'Look at me! Here I am!' and we can either pretend that it is 'out there', or we can take a serious look at ourselves.

At a social level, prisons are ghettos for one portion of our collective Shadow, as manifested in the world. Criminals kindly act out the violent, greedy, selfish, destructive and immoral aspects of ourselves, so that we can pretend those nasty qualities are 'out there', and nothing to do with us.

It used to amaze me that we treat criminals in a way which is guaranteed to perpetuate their self-image as a 'criminal' and reinforce negative beliefs about self and society, and then seem surprised at the high rate of recidivism. Yet there is an explanation for this madness. We treat criminals in a disrespectful and often dehumanising way so that they will continue to express our Shadow. To their credit, a few prisoners do manage to discover their loving, creative, expansive side — Jimmy Boyle[9] being a celebrated example — but this does break the unspoken rule. Criminals are not supposed to reveal that they are as human as the rest of us!

Likewise, most mental hospitals are carefully designed to drive people crazy, and reinforce pseudo-medical 'labelling', despite superficial appearances to the contrary. Those who have been gallant enough to 'go mad' for the rest of us are supposed to *stay* mad, otherwise it threatens our belief that craziness is 'out there'.

If we expose shadows to the night, they disappear as if by magic. However, most of us are afraid, or merely ashamed of our Shadow side — so it remains in the dark, and as we shine the light more brightly on our conscious self, the shadows deepen.

This does not mean that we should *act out* the 'dark' side of our nature. All we need do is experience and acknowledge our Shadow self, so that we no longer need to project it onto the outside world. As long as we kid ourselves that we could not even *imagine* wanting to murder someone, for example, those murderous impulses will be acted out by others, as a mirror of our Shadow. It is not enough to say the words 'I suppose I could *murder* someone'; we must *own* it within our hearts. Only when we own our Shadow can we become whole. (Those who disown their shadow often seem shallow or unreal.)

Talking of the Shadow is, of course, a convenient shorthand, since we have many Shadow selves — just as we have many Egos — and some of these selves carry our repressed *positive* qualities. Exploring our Shadow does not only reveal the gremlins of our subconscious mind; it also uncovers some sparkling gems. (I was delighted to meet two of my own positive Shadow selves in meditation — a friendly giant who represented my powerfulness, obscured by my gentle facade; and an elfin creature symbolising my magical self, which was still being suppressed by my 'scientific' beliefs.)

Since the Shadow is the complement of our conscious self, it is easy to guess what might lurk in the darkness. Which aspects of yourself do you consciously acknowledge? What are you shocked, frightened or disgusted by in others? Which qualities do you most envy in others? Which emotions do you rarely or never express? What would your opposite, your mirror-image twin be like? Therein lies your Shadow.

THE SHADOW

Picture yourself alone at night in a strange house.
Look around you, and see what you are wearing.
The wind howls outside, and beats against the
window panes. The room is dimly lit. Suddenly you
hear a rattling at the back door. Someone is there!
Someone is trying to get in! You feel afraid.
Now find yourself outside in the dark garden,
concealed behind a tree. Look at the back door. Who
is trying to get in? (It might be a familiar figure,
someone from past ages, an animal, or mythological
character. It might be anyone or anything.) Remind
yourself that this figure cannot hurt you, and approach.

When the figure turns, say 'May peace be with
you', and request to hear who it is and why it is
banging at your door. Ask what qualities in *you* it
represents. When you have finished your conversation, thank it for its help, and see a shaft of light
come out of the sky and illuminate this aspect of
your Shadow. The figure will then disappear.

Finally, move into the place it occupied, and try
to breathe in and 'own' the qualities it represented —
even though you might never choose to *express*
them. Then gently come back to the room. (This
exercise can be repeated several times to discover
other Shadow selves.)

> *Uplift yourself from your lower self, even as an*
> *elephant draws himself up from a muddy*
> *swamp.*
>
> *(The Dhammapada)*[10]

By now, your Negative Ego might be feeling a little nervous. It might be attempting to bluff its way through this chapter. 'Well, yes, I'll do these exercises when I have time, but right now I'm really rather busy.' 'Programming sounds much more fun than all this Ego and Shadow stuff.' 'I think I have good reason to feel sorry for myself!' 'I have my Ego well under control.' 'Oh, I know what's in my Shadow. I wonder what the *next* chapter is about?' *Listen to yourself*!

According to the ancient wisdom, spiritual growth involves transcending the limited and short-sighted Ego to make way for the Self. Liberation does not mean *slaying* the dragon, but rising above it, growing beyond it, seeing through its tricks and laughing gently and lovingly when it snorts fire at us. When we observe the Ego instead of hating and fighting it, we become free. When we observe the Ego instead of taking it seriously, we find inner peace. When we observe the Ego instead of identifying with it, we discover our Self.

THE SKY

Imagine yourself in a lush, green landscape, with hills rising around you. A stream flows nearby, bubbling and gurgling, and you sit beneath a large, shady tree. Use all your senses to find yourself there. Next, look up at the blue sky — and notice a small, dark cloud drifting past. Now find yourself as that cloud, looking down on the landscape, seeing the stream and the large tree. Notice a small, white, fluffy cloud not far away and become that cloud, gently moving across the sky.

Finally, become the sky. Rise above the landscape, and experience yourself as the whole sky — with clouds drifting inconsequentially through your vastness. Experience the limitlessness of being the sky .... Then gently come back to the room.

> *You do not have to destroy every cloud to see the sky,*
> *All you have to do is keep remembering you are the Sky.*
>
> *(Bartholomew)*[11]

We cannot — and should not — destroy the Ego, but we can learn to recognise, accept and move beyond it. Through knowing what happens if we empower Ego, and by understanding our payoffs, we can decide to change — to choose love rather than fear, joy rather than struggle, forgiveness rather than punishment, cooperation rather than competition, honesty rather than deception, responsibility rather than blame; and to do so every day of our lives.

5
Listening to the Whispers

Lightning flashes,
Sparks shower,
In one blink of your eye
You have missed seeing.

(Mumon)[1]

Let's suppose that your kitchen sink is blocked. The mundane world view says this is just 'one of those things', that you have unwittingly allowed vegetable peelings or food scraps to bung it up — and so you probably did. But what a barren, limited perspective! A metaphysical world view suggests that almost any event can be a 'whisper', a message, a stimulus to growth, which *you* have created — if only you would listen to yourself.

We're so brainwashed into seeing the world as random and meaningless that we can ignore countless messages from our Higher Self every day. We discover damp rising from the cellar, and dismiss it as 'bad luck'. Two light bulbs need replacing on the same day, and we say it's just 'coincidence'. A flock of seabirds lands in our garden, a hundred miles from the coast, and we call it 'curious'. Yet all of these events are metaphors, helpful signposts upon our inner journey, if we will only learn to read them. Nothing is random. Nothing is meaningless.

If you had a *dream* about a blocked sink, perhaps you would take note of its intended message. (That you are blocking up your emotions? Or refusing to let go of something you no longer need?) But when it happens in our *waking* life, we tend to dismiss such incidents as meaning-less. Yet life is a dream-metaphor, which we create just as surely as we create our dreams — and our Higher Self will often communicate through 'mundane' everyday events.

If you ignore the 'whisper' of the blocked sink, you might switch on the radio a few days later, and immediately hear of a severe traffic jam in the Dartford Tunnel. Another blockage. It's the same message again! But did you 'hear' it this time?

If these gentle whispers are not heard, your Higher Self might turn up the volume a little. After all it is yearning for you to grow. Perhaps you will suffer from a bout of constipation. Another blockage! But you decide to take some laxatives, again seeing it as a 'meaningless' incident. So your Higher Self lovingly sends you an emotional trauma, in the hope that *this* might release the blocked-up emotions. Instead, you numb yourself with tranquillisers or alcohol, or bury yourself in work. Eventually, if you continue to stubbornly ignore the message, the whispers might develop into a loud 'shout', such as bowel cancer: the same message again, several years on.

Let's take another example. Suppose you discover that your car has been clamped. The mundane world view would suggest that you've simply been foolish or unlucky, and that's all there is to it. A metaphysical world view raises the question of why you attracted that event. What were you trying to tell yourself. In what way are you 'immobi-lising' yourself, preventing yourself from moving on or changing? Perhaps you are blaming others for your stuckness, instead of taking responsibility for your own life?

If you ignore the 'whisper' of the wheel clamp, then you might choose to twist your ankle to give yourself the same message again. (This isn't to say that twisting an ankle always means that you are immobilising yourself. It might carry a myriad of different messages. Only *you* can know what your 'whispers' mean — by going within and asking.)

Another example: imagine that you buy a bar of chocolate, and later discover that you were short-changed by five pounds. Instead of allowing this to be a frustrating and pointless event, ask yourself why you created it. What is the 'whisper' from your inner self? Does it reflect your belief that you are hopelessly absent-minded? Or that people are mostly crooks? Is it a metaphor for throwing away your resources — your time, money, energy — or allowing others to take advantage of you? Perhaps you felt guilty about ignoring a charity collection, and so decided to punish yourself? Or perhaps it is an opportunity to be more philosophical, less clinging, over money? Perhaps the bar of chocolate was significant? Are you 'short-changing' yourself by eating junk food, when your inner guidance keeps whispering that you should eat a healthy diet? Or is it an opportunity for you to be assertive — to go back to the shop and request that they cash up and return your fiver? Or perhaps several of these? Which of these feels intuitively right? Which possibility sends a tingle down your spine, or gives you that 'Aha!' sensation? Which sounds painfully familiar? Which makes you feel energised?

Every event is an opportunity to learn and grow — if only we can learn to listen to the whispers; and the more we listen, the more whispers we are sent. When your Higher Self finds a way of speaking to you, it makes the most of it!

It's crucial to realise, to remember, to know, that this is not just an intriguing way of looking at our lives. It's the way our system of physical reality works. Life is not *like* a dream metaphor; it *is* a dream metaphor! Everyday events constantly mirror our inner world, offer guidance, or provide opportunities to develop personal qualities, skills and talents. Our everyday world is a truly magical oracle.

> *Not only are you*
> *the shadow*
> *that is dancing on the wall,*
> *but you are the hand*
> *that makes the shadow,*
> *and you are the light.*
>
> *(Emmanuel)*[2]

Of course, this doesn't mean that every cigarette butt on the street has a personal message just for you! The Ego clutters up our reality with a great deal of unnecessary detail, in the hope that we'll miss the 'whispers' — so we need to be discerning about what we pay attention to. Since most people still live within a mundane world view, we also need to keep a foot in *both* worlds, to stay grounded in common-sense reality, to acknowledge that 'This might sound crazy, but I think that blocked sink (or flock of seagulls, or broken light bulb) was a message to myself!'

Any strange or quirky event is sure to be a whisper. Earlier this year, I set my cassette recorder to tape Bach's Magnificat in D from an original recording. Then I sat down to meditate, with the sacred choral music playing softly in the back round. A few minutes later, I was disturbed by the sound of 'boogie-woogie' dance music coming from my tape recorder! On investigating, I found that the newly recorded cassette had inexplicably taped this lively, foot-tapping music, although the original tape was indeed Bach throughout.

I puzzled over this for a week or so, before a second whisper clarified the message. I had recorded my favourite radio serial one evening, along with twenty minutes of a programme which happened to follow it. I didn't bother to switch off the tape, and found myself listening to a religious programme, which suggested that suffering, guilt and penance is the path towards righteousness. Just as I mentally registered this message, the tape suddenly began to play 'boogie-woogie' music again! It was unmistakably the same music as before, though it was a brand new cassette.

Instantly, I got the crucial message. Spirituality is not about suffering, martyrhood, duty, worship, obligation and self-denial. It is about having fun, delighting in the wonder of life, tapping your feet to the music! God/dess has no interest in our begging for forgiveness, bearing crosses and praying to be allowed into heaven, but is urging us to dance, to celebrate, to love — to create a heaven on *earth*, where it should have been all along.

> *The light that belongs to you is the light of joy.*
> (*A Course In Miracles*)[3]

A few days after his mother died, a friend recalls that he gazed lovingly at a photograph of his mother, while pondering whether life continues after death. The thought occurred to him, 'Perhaps the end is just another beginning?' Then he sat down to watch the video of a film recorded while he was away at the funeral. The first few minutes of the film were somehow missing, but he watched it through to the end. Then, to his astonishment, the video ran on to the *beginning* of the same film — which was, of course, quite 'impossible'. The 'end' is just another 'beginning'! He got the message.

'Whispers' frequently offer practical guidance in our career, relationships and other aspects of life. A few months ago, I was invited to collaborate in a New Age book project, with several people I would have loved to work with. On the way to our initial meeting I had to change trains, and soon found that I was travelling in the wrong direction. As a result, I had to make an expensive taxi journey to arrive at the meeting on time. Since this was an uncharacteristic error, I knew it was a whisper. My Higher Self was warning me that this project, though attractive, would take me in the wrong direction, and would be a costly mistake. With a lot of misgivings, I eventually withdrew — and within weeks, as new opportunities opened up, it was clear this had been the right decision for me.

On a more light-hearted note, a friend of mine had become sexually involved with a woman he met at a party, although he confided that he had niggling doubts about the relationship. One evening, while they were dining out at a restaurant, he decided to buy some condoms from a machine. He inserted a pound coin, pushed the button and nothing emerged. Mildly irritated, he returned to the dinner table. Later that evening, they were in a pub and my friend placed a pound coin in another condom machine. Nothing happened. At this point, he remembers thinking: 'Perhaps M. and I aren't supposed to be lovers? Perhaps we should just be friends?' Then he placed another pound in the machine, pushed the button, and out came — a penny. The penny had indeed dropped! He followed his inner guidance, and the pair have since become close friends.

A client who hated her job told me she had been considering other options for two years, without taking any positive action. One day, she drove on to a roundabout, and could not figure out which exit to take. She circled three times, then thought to herself, 'Maybe I should just take any exit — at least I'll be heading somewhere.' Yet still she circled the roundabout. Suddenly, thump! A car smashed into her rear end as she dithered over which direction to take. It was a costly whisper, but she got the message. Her Higher Self was literally giving her a 'kick up the backside', encouraging her to move in *any* direction, but to *move*!

'Whispers' can also point to aspects of our inner world which need attention. Recently, while driving a friend home, I turned a corner to find the road ahead severely flooded. Instead of taking a detour, I decided it would be fun to pass through the flood, and drove towards it. Meanwhile, my friend was voicing fears and doubts: 'There might be a great hole in the road!' 'It could ruin your electrics!' I ignored him and drove on, enjoying myself. We passed through the flood safely, and later discussed the incident as a metaphor. Water is often a symbol of emotion (or the subconscious), and my desire to go through the flood symbolised my conscious willingness and desire to delve deep into my emotions. Yet my friend was 'mirroring' another aspect of myself, a part of me which was fearful and hesitant, which would prefer to 'detour' the emotional depths, a sub-personality which I needed to integrate and deal with. (I, of course, was mirroring another aspect of him.) The very existence of the flood — the fact that I had invited it into my awareness — showed that I had emotional 'work' to do.

Messages about emotional patterns are often expressed through the physical body. The body perfectly mirrors the current state of our mind and emotions. After all, we *create* our physical body, moment by moment! Bodies are not real, not 'solid stuff'; they are a trick of the light, conjured up by our own consciousness. If we accept the mundane world view — that disease has no inherent meaning or significance, that it is 'caused' by infections, viruses, heredity, biochemistry and the like, and can be 'cured' by suppressing the symptoms with drugs or removing the offending part — then we are throwing away a priceless gift, covering our ears as our Higher Self tries to speak to us.

Any symptom or illness is intended to be a source of growth. Every ache and pain, every common cold, every bout of indigestion, every headache, every broken bone has its emotional meaning, and has come to help us — if we will listen to its message. According to metaphysics, even terminal diseases can potentially be cured, by tackling the emotional blocks, imbalances and negative beliefs which are creating that illness.

Suppressed anger and resentment, for example, might re-emerge as cancer or arthritis. Suppressed love might be expressed as heart disease. Suppressed tears might be symbolised by a 'weeping' skin problem, or chronic rhinitis. Headaches usually represent an inner conflict. Neck problems might raise the question of who (or what) is a 'pain in the neck' in your life. If you suffer from constipation, perhaps you are clinging to the past? If you have cystitis, perhaps you are 'pissed off' with someone? If you are short-sighted, does this represent your reluctance to 'look ahead', to plan for the future? If you have a sore throat, are you blocking communication?

Whatever the 'whisper' from your body, ask yourself what its message, its metaphor, might be. What is the hidden emotion? What are your negative beliefs? What, if you are honest, are the 'payoffs' of having this symptom or disease? Could you give up these advantages, or achieve them in more direct and positive ways? How can you learn and grow from this illness?

*Every event that you choose for your life, no
matter how destructive, chaotic or miserable it
may seem, has been allowed to manifest because
your Wholeness has an innate knowledge of
those things you need to get you to the place
where you will choose to sink deep within, into
the stillness of who you are.*

(Bartholomew)[4]

LISTENING TO THE WHISPERS

1) Think of a situation, event or physical symptom
you have experienced in the past few days. Write
down this experience *as if it were a dream*. Try to
ignore the clutter and detail, and look for the central
themes or metaphors. Then ask yourself why you
created this experience. Was it the mirror of your
inner world — your thoughts, beliefs, desires, emotions, fears, choices or expectations? Was it guidance
from your Higher Self? Or was it an opportunity to
develop certain qualities — such as unconditional love,
forgiveness, inner peace, self-love, honesty, strength,
courage, wisdom or creativity? Or all of these?

2) In the coming weeks and months, ask yourself as
often as you can remember: 'Why am I creating this?
Is it mirror, guidance or opportunity?'

The world is a dream metaphor. We mistake it for reality
because we are so involved, so lost in the illusion, so
absorbed by the drama, that we forget we have chosen to
be here, that we are willing participants in an elaborate

stage production. Since we create our own reality, then everything 'out there' is meaningful and significant. Reality is simply a feedback mechanism which reveals our inner world. As the Upanishads state: 'What is within us is also without. What is without us is also within.' The outside world is not a fixed, solid reality, but a symbol, a means of communication, a map in our search for Oneness.

If we wish to know what we think of ourselves, we need only ask what we think of others. Buddhism teaches us to love our enemies, since they help us to grow. We have invited them into our lives as our teachers. By recognising that whatever we dislike in others is a mirror, an aspect of ourselves which we have yet to love and accept, we gain self-knowledge and move towards self-love. The more we love ourselves, the more we invite loving, caring, delightful people into our reality. As *A Course In Miracles* puts it, 'When you meet anyone, remember it is a holy encounter. As you see him, you will see yourself...'[5]

Global events, similarly, serve as mirrors of the inner world. Every news report, every global problem which we invite into our awareness — from the AIDS crisis to homelessness — carries a message, and not only a message about shifts in *world* consciousness and the need for *global* healing, but a unique *personal* message. Two people can hear the same news report, yet one 'hears' that the world is full of conflict and hatred, and another hears of the many global efforts towards love, peace and harmony. For some, the collapse of the Berlin Wall was a fearful sign that we are 'letting down our defences'; for others, it was a joyful, celebratory symbol of the healing of our divisions, the recovery of our lost wholeness.

If you choose to hear reports about terrorists and football hooligans, what is the 'whisper' about you? That you suppress your aggressive impulses? That you like to imagine you are better than those you judge and condemn? That you are afraid of yourself? 'Yes, but that's just something that happened in the outside world. It's nothing to do with me!' But you *chose* to switch on the news that day, or to hear it from a friend; and you chose to have certain thoughts in response to that news. Whatever we become aware of, we have attracted for a reason — because it can help us to learn and grow.

> To *change your world you must change your thoughts. You must become consciously aware of what you tell yourself is true every moment of the day, for that is the reality that you project outward.*
>
> (Seth)[6]

LOOKING GLASS WORLD

How do you see the world? What kind of world do you think we live in? Do you see a world full of greed, violence and hatred? Or chaos and confusion? Or a world full of love, hope and goodwill? What do you see as the most serious problems that society, or the planet, is facing at present?

When you have written down your global impressions, explore how they might mirror the way you see yourself, and the challenges you are facing in your personal and spiritual growth.

> *How many of you have been hearing whispers in*
> *your mind that you have been ignoring? ....*
> *Intuition beckons you to the future with things*
> *you feel drawn to because you love them. When*
> *you follow that voice, you will find doors*
> *opening everywhere.*
>
> *(Orin)*[7]

Since we have a vast number of probable futures open to us, we need some form of inner guidance — otherwise we would be in a constant state of indecision. This guidance often comes in the form of impulses to do this or that — to write to a friend, to read a certain book, to meditate, to go to a meeting, to buy some flowers, to sign up for an evening class. These inner 'whispers' are always creative, since they come from our inner self which is encouraging us to develop our full potential, to expand our awareness, to live more magically.

Unfortunately, we are taught to mistrust our impulses. Our culture persuades us to rely on intellect and logic when making decisions, rather than trusting intuitive hunches. We are supposed to 'think things through' before acting, and to 'control' ourselves rather than be impulsive. But by viewing the subconscious as a wild animal which must be tamed, we cut off our most valuable source of personal wisdom. As a result, impulses might be suppressed for so long that when they do eventually erupt, they can seem destructive.

Robert, aged 18, was referred to me because he had smashed several windows in a local church. He had never been in trouble before and was frightened and bewildered at his own behaviour. His parents, who were strictly religious and puritanical, saw any kind of pleasure as the road towards hellfire and damnation and forbade Robert from going to parties, wearing bright clothes, or drinking alcohol. Although he loved his parents dearly, Robert had long felt the urge to argue with them, to disagree with their view of life, to fight against his own repression. Instead, he meekly gave in to them and regularly attended church. One night, in a state of despair, he drank several cans of lager with friends from college — and on the way home, expressed years of frustration against his parents' beliefs (as well as his deep need for their love) by throwing stones at the stained glass windows.

According to Seth, impulses which are repeatedly denied will always re-emerge in one form or another. Writer Jane Roberts, who channelled Seth, says that she tended to ignore any desires which might distract her from her creative work, so she used to suppress the impulse to take physical exercise. As a result, she eventually developed a serious arthritis-like condition.

By ignoring our impulses, we not only store up trouble for ourselves, but also relinquish our power, our ability to act. 'When you are taught not to trust your impulses,' says Seth, 'you begin to lose your powers of decision, and to whatever extent involved in the circumstances, you begin to lose your sense of power because you are afraid to act.'[8]

Trusting your impulses can bring many unexpected delights. Shortly before moving to London, I spent a few days visiting ancient and mystical sites in Cornwall. One evening, I sat on the rocks at Land's End, watching the sun set across the ocean, when I felt a sudden urge to find a standing stone circle which I'd read about that day. I had only a vague idea where the circle was, but nevertheless set off towards it. After driving several miles in the fading light, I spotted a signpost which marked a public footpath, and somehow 'knew' this was the right route. The path led into a field, and I soon found myself walking more and more quickly, as though being urged to hurry by unseen forces. There was no sign of a stone circle, and I began to wonder whether I was lost — and yet I was being 'pulled' so hard that I was forced to run. I dipped down into a valley, crossed into another field — moving faster and faster — and then climbed up towards a thicket. A dark path now beckoned me through the trees. I slowed down to catch my breath, and stepped into the blackness. Moments later, a light glowed ahead of me, and I emerged into a clearing. The sight that greeted me was unforgettable.

I stood at the edge of a circle of standing stones, each eight to ten foot high, with a massive central stone which leaned at a perilous angle. The presence of the stones was quite tangible, quite awesome, and I somehow felt 'they' had given permission for me to be there. Mist hovered in the circle, luminescent in the evening light. Beyond the stones, in the West, the sunset was at its brilliant peak, streaking the sky with scarlet, pink, tangerine and purple. The mist-covered landscape swept down towards the distant sea. The scene was so magical, so stunning, that it seemed surreal. I wondered for a moment whether I was dreaming, and then silently gave thanks. Two minutes later, the sunset had grown dull, the mist no longer glowed, and darkness was fast falling. I understood why I had been urged to hurry.

GOING WITH THE FLOW

At least for the next few days, allow yourself to be
more impulsive. If you have a sudden urge to do
something — as long as it cannot harm you or others —
act on it! Do it right now, even if it interrupts
another activity.

Start listening to the subtle thoughts and feelings,
the slight shifts in energy, which bubble up from
your inner self. Try to live in the moment, rather
than planning your whole day ahead. Follow where
your energy leads you, in each and every situation.
Do something if and when it feels right. Follow your
sense of joy and enthusiasm. When you are 'going
with the flow', tasks become easy and effortless.
Trust that you have a deeper self which can handle
your day better than 'you' can, and see what happens.

LISTENING TO NATURE

Next time you are alone with nature — perhaps in a
wood, meadow, moorland, valley, clifftop or beach —
allow your mind to become very still and silent.
Begin to feel the energies around you. Become aware
that you are not alone. Everything around you is
conscious — the trees, the hills, the grass, the birds,
the sky — and all consciousness is interconnected.

Now focus your attention on whatever attracts
you — perhaps a tree, mountain, flower, stream or
rock. Say hello, and ask it to send its energy towards

you, to 'speak' to you. Be patient, but *expect* to hear, feel or sense a response. Sense your connectedness. If you are musically inclined, you might hear sounds or tones. If you are artistic, you might see patterns of light and colour. If you are literary or verbal, you might hear words. Be open to whatever comes. (This might sound bizarre, but it is a good way of learning to tune in to subtle energies which we normally ignore.)

MAKING DECISIONS

Caroline's problem was that she felt quite unable to make decisions. She worked as a secretary, and loathed it — but she couldn't decide what she really wanted to do. Her relationship with her boyfriend had lasted six years, but she was unsure whether to move in with him. At the age of 30, she still looked and behaved like a teenager. Then she began to have panic attacks. She had ignored her 'whispers' for so long that her inner self was forced to send her urgent messages. It was a desperate way of grabbing her attention.

In therapy, she realised that making almost any change was better than standing still. We learn about ourselves by making mistakes, as well as through success; we learn nothing by staying in a rut. She eventually decided to embark on a degree in business studies, and in the meantime, to move in with Jim 'to see whether to make it permanent or split up'. On making these decisions, her panic attacks stopped and were replaced by a mixture of emotions as she faced up to her fear of intimacy and commitment, and her excitement and uncertainty over becoming a mature student. She was reaching for her future.

If you dither over decision-making, over choosing which of your probable futures to reach for, or which step to take next in your personal growth, here are several ways of listening to your whispers:

* Always start with *at least three* choices. NLP (neuro-linguistic programming)[9] suggests that if we give ourselves one option, we become a robot; with two choices, we have a dilemma; but with three or more options, we have a choice. Whatever the situation, we always — *always* — have many different options, and sometimes we are stuck simply because we have not considered other alternatives. So begin by dreaming up at least three possibilities.

* Picture yourself having chosen each option in turn, and see whether it *feels* good, even if it feels scary. (Remember that a growth choice always involves taking risks.)

   Which choice would you be most proud of yourself for making? Which choice would most help you to learn and grow? Which choice(s) are based upon fear, or clinging to the familiar? Which choice would make you feel more *loving* towards yourself, others and/or the planet? Which choice(s) would make you feel smaller and more separate from others? Which choice seems filled with light and joy? Which choice increases your energy when you consider it?

* If you wish to choose between two options, 'hold' one decision in your left hand, and one in your right, and close your eyes. Tune into where your energy is shifting. Which hand is feeling warm and tingly? Which hand is feeling energised? Which hand seems to hold your attention?

* If you would like guidance, try an instant oracle such as tarot cards, I Ching, Angel Cards or PsyCards. The mundane world view suggests that the tossing of coins or yarrow stalks, or selection of cards from a pack, is random and meaningless — but metaphysics assures us that if we ask for guidance, we *will* receive it.

If you don't have an oracle, then simply open any book — a dictionary will do — and, with your eyes closed, point to a word or passage; then contemplate its possible meanings. (Of course, if you are convinced that this is nonsense, the book might mirror that belief, and give you gobbledygook. It is easy to prove ourselves right! But if you honestly ask for guidance — and are not simply giving your power away, asking for a decision to be made for you — then the reply will invariably be wise and appropriate.)

* Another approach is to use brainstorming. If you need some creative inspiration — which direction to take in your career, which city to move to, how to tackle a relationship problem, where to go on holiday — then for a maximum of twenty minutes, scribble down every idea that comes into your head. Do not censor any thoughts, however ridiculous they might sound. Write down everything. Then carefully go through your list, item by item, noting any idea which seems to leap off the page, makes you tingle or glow, or releases energy somewhere in your body.

* Dreams, of course, are a rich source of inspiration and guidance, as well as excellent training in thinking in metaphor. If you do not keep a dream diary, I strongly recommend that you give it a try. After nearly twenty years of interpreting dreams, I am still amazed at their wisdom, beauty, humour and insight — and dreams have often guided my decision-making, by mirroring unexpressed emotions and thoughts.

When I was a postgraduate student, for example, I was about to embark on a research project on a topic I'd been involved in for many years. One night, I dreamt that I was about to dive from a springboard, but the 'board' was so 'stiff' that I could not raise sufficient bounce to make my dive. When I wrote down the dream, I realised that I was already 'bored stiff' with my proposed project, and should choose another topic. My new project led me into unexplored realms of psychology which I might otherwise have ignored.

THROUGH THE GATES

(If you have to choose between two or three differ-ent options, this meditation is often helpful.) Relax deeply, then imagine yourself walking along a country lane. Use all your senses to make the scene come alive. Feel yourself striding or dawdling along. Visualise the fields and trees. Hear the birdsong. Smell the country air.

At the end of the lane, you come to three gates. Each gate represents one of your choices. (Decide before starting this visualisation which gate will correspond to which choice. You might decide that the third gate will stand for an unknown option, which you have yet to consider. If it is a simple Yes-No decision, then picture two gates.)

Look carefully at the first gate, then walk through it. (Is the gate locked? How easy is it to open? Is it a

shiny metallic gate, or a crumbling wooden one?)
What is the landscape beyond this gate? Where does
it lead to? How does it feel to be here? When you
have taken a good look around, return to the lane,
and choose another gate. Repeat the same procedure
with each gate in turn. Then gently come back to the
room.

(At one workshop, a man was trying to decide
whether or not to change his career. Gate A — which
symbolised a new career — opened into a grassy field,
and beyond it to a breathtaking cliff walk which
stretched into the distance. Gate B — pursuing his
current job in computer sales — led on to a tarmac
road, and then into a grey housing estate, ending in a
cul-de-sac. His choice could not have been more
clear.)

> *Let me be still and listen to the truth.*
>   *(A Course In Miracles)*[10]

Our strongest drive is towards rediscovering our wholeness — and however much we try to ignore it, the impulse
to grow will keep coming to the surface. Perhaps you have
always had a yearning to play the piano or flute, or run your
own business, or work abroad, or build a boat, or write
short stories, or run a marathon, or live in a country
cottage? Some of these desires might be adolescent flights
of fancy, which you never honestly wanted to happen. (The
country cottage might be a romantic ideal but perhaps you
prefer the comfort, convenience and hustle-bustle of city
life?) But other desires will be impulses which you should
act upon — impulses which will help you to grow.

Intuitive flashes about which probable future to reach for often pop up from nowhere — perhaps as images, dreams, fantasies, feelings, thoughts, impulses or bodily sensations. But whatever form intuition takes, it is completely reliable. It is a form of *knowing*. It is a message from our Higher Self.

If you do have an intuitive flash, *act on it*! If you ignore the wisdom of your Higher Self, it might not bother to speak to you for a while. Intuition will *always* guide you along your best path.

A time-honoured method for allowing intuition to blossom is to meditate regularly — whether this means taking an inner journey, dancing, walking in the woods or listening to music. Intuitive flashes often appear during or shortly after meditation. Through relaxing and stilling the mind, sinking beneath the constant chatter of the conscious self, we become more and more receptive to the whispers from our Higher Self.

Shortly after a private reading with 'Bartholomew' in Taos, New Mexico, I drove down to the nearby Rio Grande. As I sat on the riverbank, in an expanded state of consciousness after the session, I 'knew' beyond doubt that all wisdom and knowledge was available to me. I simply had to ask. I posed questions about my higher purpose, past lifetimes, karmic links with others, and probable futures — and answers came flooding into my mind. An unusual bird flew past, so I asked what it was — and an inner voice told me. Sadly, I quickly returned to 'normal' but the sense of having potential *access* to all knowledge has remained. Whatever we wish to know — however trivial, however important — *is* available in an energy field that constantly surrounds us. We only have to ask, trust, sink into our inner stillness — and listen to the whispers.

6
What is Really Real?

The fly that touches honey cannot use its wings;
so the soul that clings to spiritual sweetness
ruins its freedom and hinders contemplation.
(*St. John of the Cross*)[1]

In her enchanting story of *The Velveteen Rabbit*, Margery
Williams[2] tells of a cloth rabbit who longs to be more than
just a toy. Scorned by the more expensive and mechanical
toys, the shy young rabbit feels very second-rate and
insignificant. However, he is told by the wise old Skin
Horse that, while some toys are destined to remain toys
forever, some playthings can be magically transformed — and
become Real. The secret ingredient is love. When a child
loves you for a long, long time, says the Skin Horse, then
you gradually become Real. And once you are Real, you
will live forever....

If reality is an illusion that we create — no more 'real' than
Middle Earth or Valhalla — then it raises an important
question. What is *really* Real? As we probe deeper and
deeper into the universe, what *really* exists? The ultimate
answer seems to be Love. Love is everything that is really
real. Love is the Grand Unified Force; and, just as when
we watch a good movie, we might become so emotionally
involved that we forget it is 'only a movie', it is our *feelings*
which make life appear to be so real.

Sadly, we are taught to look upon emotions as some kind
of social disease. 'Nice' people — saintly people — simply don't
have them. Oh, they might smile serenely, and perhaps

express compassion, but they never get angry, or excited, or tearful, or passionate. They are detached from anything as lowly and demeaning as human feelings. Spiritual growth, apparently, means behaving like a robot!

The truth is that strong feelings are scary. Emotions create too much of a mess in our neat, tidy, rational world — and so we learn to squash them. We might sit on our anger, our sadness, our jealousy, our resentment, our fears, our hurt — even our love, joy and exuberance. (When asked how we are feeling, how often do we shrug our shoulders and say 'Well, OK, I suppose'?) We have almost forgotten how to feel.

The problem is that suppressing emotions is not only unsaintly; it is downright dangerous. 'Emotions,' says Seth, 'flow through you like storm clouds or blue skies, and you should be open to them and react to them. You are not your emotions. They flow through you. You feel them. And then they disappear. When you attempt to hold them back, you build them up like mountains.'[3] And those mountains are volcanic. They will eventually erupt.

Every time we laugh when we are hurt, or smile when we feel angry, it is like burying an unripe fruit inside us. Instead of ripening into an edible delight, the emotion begins to rot and decay and eventually its poison spreads throughout our body, often re-emerging as illness and disease.

What is more, emotions are a crucial aspect of how we create our reality. Thoughts set up a resonance which attracts certain events, people and situations into our lives, while the strength of our emotions determines *how rapidly* we attract events. Lazaris[4] suggests that if we experience the full depth and intensity of our emotions — not just so-called 'negative' emotions such as anger, fear and hurt, but also 'positive' emotions such as joy, love and enthusiasm — it creates a powerful force-field, which can attract miraculous success into our lives.

Emotions are not good or bad, positive or negative; they simply *are*. They become destructive only if they are suppressed and denied. It is not the *emotion* which is negative, but the fact that it has been squelched. Stuffing down our emotions only makes them more powerful. It is like taking out a mortgage: we have to repay the loan many times over. Why bother, when we could so easily pay in cash?

As soon as we fully *experience* an emotion, it changes. It leads us towards inner peace. By accepting it, by wrapping it in a warm blanket of love, by flowing with it, we begin to release and transform it. It is far more painful and exhausting to suppress our emotions than it is to experience them. It is the struggle to *suppress* our pain which really hurts.

Nothing changes through being hated or denied. Paradoxically, it is only when we accept ourselves *as we are* that we begin to change. Emotions are part of our wholeness. By *welcoming* each and every emotion — making no judgements about how we 'should' or 'should not' feel — we allow ourselves to grow and change.

> Go to the feelings, and in the acceptance of the
> feelings, the release begins …. The emotion
> comes and goes. What you need is the willing-
> ness to sit with yourself and discover this.
>
> (Bartholomew)[5]

YOUR EMOTIONS

1) Which feelings do you habitually suppress, or deny having at all? Consider how you handle each of the following emotions. Do you express them openly and honestly — at least to yourself? Or stuff them down? Or sit on them until you explode? Or completely block them from awareness? Do you handle these emotions better in some situations than in others? Which feelings do you have most difficulty with? Which feel most painful or scary? Which situations tend to arouse these emotions in you? What are your beliefs about these emotions?

Anger	Love
Affection	Resentment
Jealousy	Passion
Lust	Envy
Sadness	Enthusiasm
Compassion	Grief
Irritation	Happiness
Hurt	Self-pity
Joy	Guilt
Disappointment	Shame
Embarrassment	Fear

2) Where do your suppressed emotions go? In what form do they re-emerge? As physical symptoms? Or feeling anxious or depressed? Or do you project your emotions onto the outside world — seeing your fears, anger, sadness or envy in other people, or in the world at large? How are your hidden emotions affecting your life? What is the price you are paying?

ANGER

Anger can be a liberating form of self-assertion, and a powerful motivator for change, when expressed in a constructive and appropriate way. However, it is an emotion that leads many of us to play games — either by denying we feel angry, or by squashing it in an effort to be seen as reasonable, easygoing and likeable, or from fear of being rejected.

Getting angry is often linked with being 'bad-tempered', 'out of control' or even aggressive. But it only explodes into violence when it has been suppressed. It is not anger that causes violence, but the attempt to block it! Denied anger has to go somewhere; it cannot simply vanish into the air. So it eventually re-emerges as violent aggression or as physical disease, depression, 'accidents' or other traumas. Unless we release our emotions, they tend to create unpleasant realities.

Matthew grew up in a family atmosphere of sweetness and light. His parents never exchanged a cross word. If there was a difference of opinion, they would hurriedly remedy the situation by changing the subject. Conflicts were never even acknowledged, let alone resolved. Throughout his childhood, Matthew can recall feeling angry just once — when his father unwittingly trod on a model boat which Matthew had spent several weeks constructing. Believing that he had no 'right' to be angry over this mishap, Matthew retreated to his bedroom, took out a penknife and cut a painful slit in his own hand.

Matthew married a woman who came from a highly volatile family. He was fascinated — and frightened — by Marianne's ability to express her feelings so openly. She, in turn, welcomed his calm quiet manner which seemed so restful after the hubbub of her childhood. Within a few years, however, Marianne had grown weary of Matthew's only emotion being bland 'OK-ness' and had a brief but passionate affair. When she admitted the affair to Matthew, hoping for a display of anger or jealousy, he meekly *apologised* for not being good enough for her and promised to try harder in future. With that he left the room; end of conversation. End of marriage. Marianne, outraged by his response, promptly packed her bags and left — leaving Matthew bewildered and confused.

Two years later, Marianne remarried and Matthew plunged into depression. In group therapy, I suggested that Matthew might re-play the final scene from his marriage, *as if* he were someone who expressed anger openly. He chose to do this by re-writing the scene in the form of a script for a play. In the first draft, however, the male character exploded with rage and hit Marianne across the face. Although this showed that Matthew's anger was not far beneath the surface, it also revealed his belief that anger is dangerous, so I encouraged him to try again. This time, the couple still shouted at each other, but were open and honest about how they felt. We enacted this scene, scripts in hand, during a therapy session — and for the first time, Matthew felt angry with Marianne. As he released his anger, he felt his love for his ex-wife, and wept over their divorce. Over the weeks, as Matthew experienced his tangle of emotions, his depression lifted.

Anger should be a constructive force based upon self-love and self-respect. But while we suppress our anger, it will appear 'out there' in the world, in other people. Like Matthew, we will keep creating realities which coax or provoke us into feeling anger — by being hurt, by suffering from injustice, by seeing a world full of hatred and cruelty. The more we block anger, the more destructive it becomes in our reality.

Hang on a minute ... If we create our own reality, then how can we ever be *justified* in feeling angry? Whatever happens, we created it. Right, and after we have released our anger, the next step is to work out why we created that situation, and which beliefs and thoughts support our anger. But we cannot skip to this stage until our anger has been expressed.

Feelings do not have to be 'justified'; they do not have to be rational; they should never be judged as OK or not OK, or covered up with positive thoughts and affirmations. *Feelings simply are*, and they must be expressed and released in some appropriate way.

YOUR ANGER

Make a list of five incidents from your past which still make you angry. Release the anger now — perhaps writing down what happened, and how you felt. Or by pummelling a pillow or cushion to express your rage. (If you are not in touch with your anger, fake it! Punch a pillow *as if* you were angry, until the feelings surface.) Or write a letter to the person concerned, being totally open and honest about your feelings — and then burn it. (Resist the temptation to post it. The problem is *your* anger, not what the other person did.) Or, if anger is still spoiling your relationship with someone, then consider expressing your feelings directly to them, even if the incident occurred some years ago. Also examine the beliefs which caused your anger in that situation.

Then think about *why* you suppress your anger. What are your payoffs? Does it make you feel 'better than'? Does it feed your martyr? Do you believe that anger is destructive? Do you tell yourself you have no right to feel angry? Or live by the maxim 'anything for the sake of peace'? What are the costs of blocking your anger? (Low self-esteem? Physical symptoms? Depression? Shallow, unsatisfying relationships? Inability to assert yourself?)

Finally, re-write each incident. 'Rewind the film', and visualise what you *wish* you had said and done in that situation. Write yourself a new script in which you are open ¬nd honest about your anger. Then look out for your next opportunity to express anger in a constructive way.

GRIEF

Grief is another emotion — or rather, set of emotions — which often creates problems. Whenever we suffer a major loss in our lives — such as the death of a loved one, divorce, redundancy, miscarriage, children leaving home, or the end of a love affair — we need to go through a period of mourning. Grieving might involve feeling sadness, yearning, fear, guilt, anger and even despair — and all too often, we try to suppress these emotions, because they are so intense and painful. Many people believe that if they can just get through the days, time will heal the wounds.

Unfortunately, time alone does not heal. It is expressing and releasing the emotions that heals. Crying, sobbing and raging are essential to the healing process. The more we suppress our grief, the longer it continues — and it will often re-emerge, years later, as depression or physical disease. Even when we go through *welcome* transitions — such as getting married, moving house or having a baby — we need to mourn our former life.

Betty, aged 43, was severely depressed when I first met her. She had been treated with drugs, which made her feel worse, and found it difficult to speak at all. After an almost silent session, I felt unsure how to begin to help her; so I asked her if she could draw a picture of a tree. Slowly, a drawing emerged of a yew tree, overlooking several gravestones. A clue to her problem at last. I asked Betty who lay in the graves. 'Children' she told me. Gently, I said I wondered whether she had lost a child, whether that was why she was so unhappy. After a long pause, she nodded and the story emerged of a stillbirth she had experienced in her early twenties. Betty had never seen the baby, blamed herself for its death, and was still grieving. Several weeks later, on the twenty-first anniversary of the baby's death, we held a tearful and moving ceremony with candles and poetry, in which Betty said goodbye to her baby and gave herself permission to get on with the rest of her life.

HURT

> *You add suffering to the world just as much*
> *when you take offence as when you give offence.*
> (*Ken Keyes*)[6]

Creating our own reality is sometimes interpreted as meaning that we cannot hurt people unless they allow us to do so. At one level, that is true. But we do have impact on other people. Metaphysics always *gives* us responsibility. It never takes it away. It never allows us to blame others, or avoid responsibility for our own actions. If we hurt someone, we *must* take responsibility for it.

Lazaris suggests that hurting someone — consciously causing distress — is *always* manipulative; it is always dishonest. We never hurt someone by being honest and genuine. What is more, hurt is highly destructive. It erodes love and trust; it rips our self-esteem, self-love, self-confidence and identity. It is the only emotion that takes *time* to heal. According to Lazaris, it is very dangerous to play games with hurt — hurting others, squashing our hurt, pretending to be hurt when we feel angry — 'more dangerous than you know'.[7]

Emily felt hurt and betrayed by a close friend who had borrowed a considerable sum of money towards down-payment on a house and then, when Emily eventually enquired about repayment, angrily claimed that she thought the money had been a gift. Her 'friend' abruptly broke off all contact. Although Emily knew that her friend had been manipulative, she wondered whether she herself had been selfish, and should have forgotten about the loan. She struggled with her anger and guilt for nearly a year, and had gradually resolved these feelings. But she was left with a deep sense of hurt over her friend's behaviour and had been unable to trust anyone since then.

One evening, Emily set aside some time when she could be alone. She took the phone off the hook, and threw herself into her hurt. She wept and sobbed. She 'spoke' to her ex-friend. She writhed about on the floor in agony. She re-lived similar hurts from childhood. Then, after half an hour, feeling exhausted but relieved, she stopped — and soaked in a perfumed bath with a magazine. The next day, she realised that the memory had lost its sting at last. Then she felt ready to look at why she had created that situation.

If someone hurts us, then we need to express and release our hurt, anger and sadness. *Then* we should look at why we created that reality. What were our negative beliefs? What are our payoffs? Why did we respond in the way that we did? What are the thoughts and beliefs that support this emotion? What can we learn from this experience?

> *We never get upset over what happens. Never.*
> *We get upset because of preconceived ideas as to*
> *what we think should happen, what we want to*
> *happen.*
>
> *(Vernon Howard)*[8]

GUILT

Guilt is another painful and troublesome feeling. Its original function, according to Seth, was to make us feel bad, by briefly separating us from our sense of love and connectedness, so that we would not *repeat* a harmful act. It was not designed to *punish* us. It was simply a preventive measure.

Unfortunately, the Ego has made a monopoly of guilt, seeing it as a splendid excuse for misery and martyrdom. Nowadays, people do not just feel guilty over causing *hurt*. We might indulge in 'feeling guilty' about having a lazy Sunday in bed, splashing out on new clothes, making love, eating a large slice of chocolate gateau with lashings of cream, and other completely harmless and enjoyable experiences! The puritanical Ego believes we should always pay for having fun. After all, life is supposed to be a struggle!

The Ego revels in guilt, since it is a way of clinging to the past, and hanging on to old payoffs. 'I can't possibly allow myself to be happy now, because I had an affair/ caused a car crash/stole some money/had sex with my brother or sister/was cruel to my dog/betrayed my best friend — five, ten or twenty years ago. So, in the meantime, I'll just see how dreadful a time I can have, so that everyone feels sorry for me and I can avoid taking responsibility for my life!' (If this makes you squirm, or giggle nervously, you have just recognised yourself!)

A Course In Miracles repeatedly insists that there is no sin, only error. We make mistakes through ignorance, fear, negative beliefs and misdirected love — not because we are evil or sinful. Sin is an invention of the Ego, which readily plays 'less than' games: 'Horrible me! Awful me! What terrible things I have done! What a miserable earthworm I am!' Guilt is a sign of our refusal to love ourselves, a symbol of our desire to be separate from All That Is. It blocks our personal and spiritual growth. 'Guilt is more than merely not of God' says *A Course*. 'It is the symbol of attack on God.'[9] ('Oh goody,' says the Ego, 'I can feel guilty about feeling guilty now!')

> *It is not that you have to be 'good', just stop believing you are 'bad'.*
>
> *(Bartholomew)*[10]

It is the Ego that suggests that, because there are people starving in the world, we should feel guilty about having more than we need — as if our guilt will somehow fill those hungry mouths. It is Ego which drives us to be dutiful and fulfil false obligations. It is Ego that thinks we should constantly fret about our family and the future, in case God decides we are taking life for granted, and hurls down a bolt of lightning. The Ego imagines that it is somehow being empathic to increase the suffering in the world by adding our own. ('Why should I be happy when others are miserable?')

Most guilt can be understood as hidden resentment. Guilt is not a true emotion; it is a cover-up for other feelings which we feel we shouldn't have. Whenever we feel guilty, it is worth asking ourselves why we feel angry and resentful. Our resentment does not need to be understandable or 'rational'; it simply needs to be expressed and released.

Guilt can also be a form of self-punishment — anger turned against the self, in the absence of self-love and self-forgiveness. All too often, it is also a form of manipulation — a way of hurting or punishing others, or persuading them to do what we want, in the absence of honesty and integrity. Guilt does nothing but harm.

YOUR GUILT

If you suffer from guilt, write down what you feel guilty or ashamed about. (If you are reluctant to commit yourself to paper, speak to yourself in a mirror.) You do not need to confess to anyone else. Just be honest with *yourself*. What are your shameful secrets? What are the dastardly deeds, thoughts and fantasies which your Negative Ego pokes and taunts you with?

Now examine your list. What is the hidden resentment that lies beneath your guilt? Who are you angry with? Who are you trying to manipulate? Is your guilt based upon a belief that you should not have fun, or that your body is not your own, or that you are not allowed to feel angry, or assert your own needs? If so, perhaps you should reassess those beliefs.

If your guilt is due to harming others — or harming yourself — then try to *understand* why you behaved as you did. What were your negative beliefs, thoughts and fears? Were you acting from your inner Child's desperate desire for love? Or your inner Adolescent's need to be in control, or to be understood? (See *Into the Shadowlands*.) What are your Ego's payoffs for clinging to guilt?

Now — forgive yourself. Don't let your Ego convince you that your mistakes are so 'special' that they are unforgivable. ('No-one has done anything as awful as *me*!' Who are you kidding?) Understand, and forgive yourself. Release yourself from the past.

FEAR

> *Fear*
> *is only looking in the mirror*
> *and making faces*
> *at oneself*
>
> *(Emmanuel)*[11]

Reality is just a complex holographic illusion that we create. There is nothing to fear. Yet how many of us are paralysed by our fears? Fear of rejection. Fear of humiliation. Fear of failure. Fear of success. Fear of intimacy. Fear of commitment. Fear of caring. Fear of being vulnerable. Fear of getting hurt. Fear of loving. Fear of being loved. Fear of being unloved. Fear of loneliness. Fear of loss. Fear of making mistakes. Fear of being found out. Fear of thinking for ourselves. Fear of change. Fear of freedom. Fear of responsibility. Fear of the unknown. Fear of cancer. Fear of nuclear war. Fear of financial problems. Fear of violent crime. Fear of our emotions. Fear of fear itself.

According to Lazaris, fear is highly repetitive; our greatest fears now will probably be the same fears we had ten or twenty years ago, and even many lifetimes ago.[12] However, he suggests that fear does have a useful function. Whereas love is the accelerator which gets us moving, fear is the brake which prevents us going in the wrong direction. It can help us to steer a steady course through life. But if we react too strongly to fear, the brake is applied so hard that we come to a standstill, and fail to grow — which means a wasted lifetime.

Perhaps the most basic human fear is that of loneliness or separation — a fear so great that many people will endure loveless and even abusive relationships, rather than face living alone. Yet mystics have been saying for thousands of years that we are all aspects of a greater whole — that our separateness is an illusion, that we are ultimately One. It is our *illusion* of separateness which lies at the root of our fears. As it states in the Upanishads, 'Wherever there is other, there is fear.' If we realised that we are all One, and that the only true reality is Love, how could we ever be lonely or afraid?

The trick of overcoming fear is not to stop feeling frightened, but to act *in spite of* our fear — in the catchphrase of Susan Jeffers' self-help book, *Feel The Fear And Do It Anyway*! For example, *everyone* is scared of intimacy. Some people allow this fear to block them from forming close relationships of any kind; while others face the challenge of deep intimacy despite their fears. Fear of death means that the most dangerous activity which many of us will contemplate is crossing the road; while others, no less afraid of death, will canoe down dangerous rapids, explore the wildest of jungles, or whizz around motorcycle tracks. It is not fear that impedes us, but how we *handle* our fears.

(Personally, I find that labelling fear as 'excitement' enables me to tackle almost anything.)

Every day, we can make choices based upon our fears or choices based upon our desire for growth. If we do not face up to our fears, we might project them onto the outside world, perhaps in the form of violent crime, epidemics, disasters or a vengeful God, or (closer to home) in the form of a partner, family or friends who 'block' our growth, and thus protect us from facing our fears.

YOUR FEAR

1) Check through the various fears listed above. Which of these have blocked your growth? Where have you allowed fear to reign? How might life have been different if you hadn't been afraid?

Now look at which fears prevent you from doing what you want to do now. Which fears stand in the way of your Dreams for the future? Or block you from developing personal qualities, talents or skills? Or prevent you from finding inner peace? Which 'fear choices' do you need to replace with 'growth choices'?

What are your payoffs for letting these fears overcome you? Avoiding adult responsibility? Avoiding the challenge of growth? Feeling 'better than' or 'less than'? Blaming or manipulating others? Rationalising and justifying your behaviour? Feeling sorry for yourself?

What are the negative beliefs — about yourself, other people or the world — which underlie your fears?

2) For each fear, visualise a worst-case scenario of
'what might happen' — *and how you would
handle it*. (Our tendency is to suppress our worst
fears, because we feel sure we would not even
survive, let alone *cope* with the situation!) Imagine
feeling foolish, and a crowd of people laughing at
you. Imagine being told that you have cancer.
Imagine failing your examinations. Or losing your
temper at work. Or being made bankrupt. And
watch yourself handling it, even learning from it.

Then tell your subconscious that you do not wish
to create that negative reality. Allow the traumatic
scene to turn into a photograph, which you cut up
with scissors and burn. Finally, visualise the positive
outcome that you desire: perhaps confirmation that
you are 100 per cent fit, that you have passed your
exams, or that your finances are secure.

OVERCOMING FEAR

Relax deeply, then imagine yourself on a mountain
path. Look around at the landscape. Feel your feet
on the ground. Listen to the sounds. Smell the air.
Walk along the path, as it winds its way up into the
mountain. Eventually, you turn a corner and notice a
cave ahead of you. As you approach the cave, you
notice that someone is there. It might be an old man,
or an old woman. Let it be whoever it is.

Greet the wise one, and talk to them of the fears
that you wish to overcome. You will be given one or
more gifts — gifts which symbolise the personal

qualities you need to develop in order to overcome
your fears. (Perhaps honesty, integrity, courage,
trust, gratitude, humour, creativity, wisdom or love.)
Accept each gift, allowing yourself to see it, know
what it symbolises, and understand its message. If
you are not sure, then ask. Then thank the wise one,
and say goodbye.

Now turn and retrace your steps down the
mountain path, carrying your gifts. Then gently
come back to the room, (Next time you face a
situation in which fear blocks you, remind yourself
of your gifts — and use them.)

Fear is the other side of love
Fear is the dread of love
Fear is the dread of losing
what we have and are
of letting go in order to
become what will be
We are afraid of love
Love demands all we are

(Miller Mair)[13]

LOVE

Many people believe that they would love themselves if
only someone else would love them *first*! But our relationships with other people — whether partner, friends, relatives
or colleagues — can only mirror our relationship with
ourselves. The world is our mirror. If we look at our
relationships with others, we merely see a reflection of our
love (or lack of love) for ourselves.

The Ego is afraid of love. It only seeks relationships in

order to *be loved*. It gives in hope of receiving. It yearns to feel 'special' to someone, to nourish its self-importance or relieve its sense of inferiority. It does not want intimacy in order to *love*, in order to grow. In fact, it does not desire *intimacy* at all. It prefers the idea of 'romance', or *searching* for love. For the Ego, it is highly dangerous to get too close to anyone.

Ego-based relationships, whether with friends or partners, tend to be characterised by a need for security or a search for self-esteem. Some of the telltale signs might be:
- idolising the other person
- feeling desperate for love
- a high degree of dependency
- fear of being alone
- seeking the other's approval
- resenting the other person having their own friends
- feeling trapped
- lack of emotional intimacy
- lack of respect for each other
- concern with the social status of one's partner/friend
- having affairs
- feeling oppressed by the other
- wanting to be 'special' to the other person
- a sense of futility or disappointment
- feeling anxious and insecure
- jealousy and possessiveness
- dishonesty and manipulation
- worrying whether the relationship will last
- not growing as separate individuals
- expecting the other to be the solution to life's problems
- a secure, stable but dull relationship
- wanting a partner to be your 'missing half'

Deborah's parents had had a tumultuous relationship in which frequent violent arguments would be followed by tender love scenes. She grew up associating 'love' with an emotional roller-coaster, and although she was looking for a long-term partner, Deborah quickly became bored and dissatisfied in a stable relationship. She was hooked on 'falling in love', on the emotional highs and lows of fresh romance. As soon as she felt secure in a relationship, she began to feel restless and uneasy.

Tom, likewise, was not searching for love. His only desire was for security. He was quite bemused by his wife's dissatisfaction with their empty, shallow and predictable relationship. 'I work hard. I give her all my money. I would never be unfaithful,' he shrugged. 'What more does she want?' For Tom, intimacy meant having sex twice a week. Marriage was an excuse to stop growing.

Tom and Deborah were both allowing their Ego to control their relationships. The Ego likes to be stroked. It favours whatever is safe and familiar. It feels most comfortable if the present merely repeats the past. 'Better the devil you know,' says Ego. If true love should knock on the door, Ego will coolly slip the bolt and pretend to be out.

If you really want a loving, supportive and intimate relationship, you will already have one. After all, we create our own reality. We always get what we want. As soon as we are ready and willing, there it is! It is only because of our fears and hidden agendas that we don't always get what we *think* we want.

Loving, intimate relationships do provide endless opportunities for growth. Our loved ones will often be people we have known over many lifetimes, who have agreed to play a role which will help us to learn and grow — perhaps by recreating a childhood pattern, by rousing our hidden emotions, by challenging us to remain open, honest and loving, or by modelling qualities which we need to develop. We choose the perfect partners for whatever we wish to learn.

Intimacy brings all of our unresolved conflicts, suppressed emotions and hidden agendas to the surface to be healed, and a partner provides an ideal mirror in which to gaze at parts of our own Shadow and rediscover our wholeness.

Sexuality, likewise, can be a wonderful vehicle for personal and spiritual growth. For centuries, most religious traditions have debased sex — seeing it as dirty and sinful, or purely for procreation — and have advocated celibacy as a path towards God. Yet when we truly 'make love' — as opposed to merely having sex — our souls, our spiritual essences merge. Making love is a metaphysical experience in which our Ego boundaries are lost, our fears of intimacy and vulnerability overcome. When we make love, we briefly glimpse and touch our Oneness with another. We learn not only to give and receive love, but to *become* Love.

Relationships (of any kind) which are based upon love, rather than upon the need for security or self-esteem, are marked by:

- openness
- honesty
- vulnerability
- responsiveness
- trust
- depth of sharing and intimacy
- ability to resolve conflict
- listening
- caring

- giving
- mutual respect
- shared values and attitudes
- shared Dreams
- commitment
- having fun
- forever learning about each other
- being embedded in a social network
- encouraging each other to grow and change
- unconditional love and acceptance
- being two whole individuals

> *To whatever degree you have placed the respon-*
> *sibility for your feelings of love and wholeness*
> *on someone else, is the degree to which you are*
> *bound to disappointment.*
>
> *(Bartholomew)*[14]

YOUR LOVE

1) Think about the closest relationships in your life —
past and present. Are they based upon the need for
security? Or a search for approval and self-esteem?
Or genuine love and caring? (Or a mixture of these?)
2) Consider the characteristics of a loving relationship listed above. How many of these are part of
your closest relationship — whether with a partner,
friend or relative? What could you do to make this
relationship more loving?
3) Look for opportunities to be more loving each day
— not just with your loved ones, but in every moment
of the day. How can you be more loving towards

yourself today? How might you be more loving at work? Or while shopping? While doing household chores? Or during leisure activities? How much love can you pour into your life?

HEALING A RELATIONSHIP

If you have a problem with a friend, partner, child, colleague or neighbour, try meeting them on the inner planes before discussing the issue with them in person:

Relax deeply, then imagine you are on a grassy riverbank. Use all your senses to find yourself there. Now begin to breathe in white light (or whatever colour feels appropriate) until you are radiating light. You are becoming your Higher Self. You are now able to see the problem from a higher perspective, knowing that you have created it for a reason.

Now imagine the other person walking slowly towards you. With each step, they are becoming more and more radiant with light. You can now speak from your Higher Self to the other person's Higher Self. Speak from your heart. Speak from love. Listen lovingly for their reply. Understand the lesson in this for you, and heal the rift between you. Then gently come back to the room. (When you later discuss the problem face-to-face, you might be amazed at the telepathic impact of this meditation.)

RELEASING A RELATIONSHIP

1) If you find yourself yearning for a relationship
with someone where the feelings are not mutual, or
the other person's love has died, ask yourself what
aspect of you that person represents. What qualities
are you projecting on to them, which you need to
reclaim as part of your wholeness? Strength? Talent?
Practicality? Beauty? Intelligence? Intuition? Emotionality? Compassion? Creativity? Playfulness? Spontaneity? Humour?

What are your payoffs for clinging to this relationship? Self-pity? Martyrdom? Avoidance of
intimacy? Clinging to the past? Re-creating a painful
relationship from your childhood, in hope of healing
the wounds? What do you need to learn from this
situation, so that you can let go?

2) Relax deeply, then imagine you are in a lush,
green meadow. Feel the warmth of the sun. Hear the
birdsong. Touch the grass. Smell the wild flowers.

Now ask to meet the part of you which refuses to
let go of this relationship — and watch as this sub-
personality approaches. (It might be a child, or
teenager, or of the opposite sex. Let it be whoever it
is.) Find out why this part of you is clinging to this
relationship. What is it trying to do for you? Now
explain why it is necessary to let go, so that you can
move on. (If necessary, allow yourself to become this
sub-personality, and experience the hurt, sadness,
anger or other emotions he or she is holding.) Then
merge with that aspect of yourself.

When you are ready, the person you have been yearning for will enter the meadow, and approach you. Explain that you are now ready to let go. Give them a hug and say 'I love you enough to set you free. I love myself enough to let go.' See a cord joining you, from their solar plexus to yours — and cut the cord with a knife. Then choose to walk away — and gently come back to the room.

Love is the doorway to enlightenment.

(Orin)[15]

Love is all that is really Real. Love is the antidote to fear. Love transforms every emotion. Love is what we are, and what we are becoming — however hard we might resist it! Whereas the Ego seeks to divide and separate, love seeks to unify and heal. Love is the realisation of Oneness. Or as Seth pithily puts it, 'The whole is the sum of its hearts.'[16]

Love might seem an airy-fairy, romantic, idealistic concept — all very well for weekends and holidays, but not very relevant to our everyday, toast-and-marmalade, bills-and-office-lunch reality. But love *can* become part of every moment of our lives. Love is not just about intimate, sexual relationships, but about *all* of our relationships: our relationship with self, with friends, with family, with colleagues, with strangers, with animals, with nature, with possessions, with money, with our work, with our body, with ideas, with the planet, with our Dreams, with All That Is.

If we loved ourselves unconditionally, then we would create a totally loving and joyous reality — quite automatically. Every fear, every limitation, every hurt, every trauma, every problem, every shadow that we see in the world 'out there' reflects our lack of self-love. Whatever we crave from others — love, freedom, respect, pleasure, approval, appreciation — is what we need to give ourselves.

Until we love ourselves, we cannot love anyone else. (We might 'need' someone, cling to them, romanticise them, pity them, idealise them — but we cannot *love* them unless we love ourselves.) Metaphysical techniques are just interim measures while we are learning to love. The power does not lie in the techniques, but in love.

At the first personal growth workshop I ever attended, I still recall an exercise in which we had to write down our faults and weaknesses, what we disliked about ourselves. No problem! The room immediately buzzed with activity as we all scribbled down voluminous notes. Next, we were asked to list our strengths, what we really loved about ourselves. A hush fell over the room. Brows were furrowed and pencils licked, as people struggled over their empty sheet of paper. Looking rather sheepish, we hesitantly listed one or two points, worrying that we might sound narcissistic or arrogant. We are taught that we should not love ourselves — that self-love is conceited, vain or selfish — and obediently, we learn to dislike and criticise ourselves. As Louise Hay[17] points out, we do this all the time — and it gets us nowhere.

SELF-LOVE

1) What makes you so unlovable? What are the faults, characteristics, misdeeds and imperfections which you use as excuses for not loving yourself? Make a list. If a friend gave you this list of reasons why they could not love themselves, what would you say?

Now write down some affirmations, using your
list of 'faults':
'I love myself while being moody and bad-tempered.'
'I love myself while being critical and judgemental.'
'I love myself while being nervous and timid.'
'I love myself while being lazy.'
(This does not mean that you must love *being*
nervous or critical; just that you must love *yourself*
— whatever your Ego is up to.)

2) How would your life be different if you were your
own best friend — if you loved yourself unconditionally? In what ways would you change what you do,
say, think, feel and believe? Would you make different choices and decisions about how to organise your
daily life? Or have different Dreams for the future?
(Spend time over this exercise. Don't pretend that
you already love yourself totally. If you did, you
wouldn't be here!)

From now on — in whatever ways feel possible —
begin to act 'as if' you were your own best friend.

Self-love does not mean loving only your good points, or
loving the person you are becoming, or believing you are
perfect. It simply means loving and accepting yourself
unconditionally *as you are*. Right now — including the fact
that you are unable to love yourself! Many of us secretly
think we will love ourselves when we have resolved a
certain problem, or when we are successful, or when we
are less busy, or when we are older, or when we are in a
loving relationship — but tomorrow never comes. Loving
ourselves has to come first.

'But I don't deserve to be loved.' We don't have to deserve

it — we just have to be willing to *do* it! As we learn to love, everything else in life will naturally fall into place: relationships, work, money, health, success, joy. 'But I don't deserve that either' says Ego. Just be willing!

> *If you stop trying to become whatever it is you*
> *are trying to become and instead have the feeling*
> *that you are what you are, and* this *is the*
> *moment — your struggle stops.*
>
> *(Bartholomew)*[18]

7

Into the Shadowlands

Now as I was young and easy under the apple boughs
About the lilting house and happy as the grass was green,
The night above the dingle starry,
Time let me hail and climb
Golden in the heydays of his eyes ...

(Dylan Thomas)[1]

Picture a large, sunlit yellow room — a child's nursery. A brightly painted rocking horse, with flowing mane, neighs as it gently rocks to and fro. Laughing clowns pop up out of rainbow-coloured boxes. Clockwork trains, wound by invisible hands, circle their way through sugar-pink mountains. Books open of their own accord, whispering tales of unicorns, mermaids, fairies and enchanted forests. A sandy-coloured bear, its fur cuddled to baldness, pours tea and hands out tiny sandwiches at a teddy bears' picnic. A musical box plays its charming melody. Sparks of light flash and twinkle in the air. It is a room which brims with magic and delight.

As you imagine this, you might become aware that you are no longer alone. Peeking over your shoulder, perhaps rather shyly, is a wide-eyed, playful Child, four or five years of age — gazing in awe and wonder at this magical nursery. This is the Child within you. This Child is not a figment of your imagination, not just an interesting concept, but a flesh-and-blood conscious being, very much 'alive' in the here-and-now. The Child within can make or break our lives.

Metaphysics — along with transactional analysis, Gestalt therapy, psychosynthesis, hypnotherapy and so on — suggests that we have many different selves. Each self is a sub-personality in its own right, with its own characteristic ways of behaving, thinking and feeling. Each might have its own beliefs, values, attitudes, payoffs and hidden agendas. Whenever we say 'On the one hand, I ... but on the other hand ...', we are experiencing two of our inner selves; and this is *perfectly normal*. It is not a sign that we are crazy or neurotic. *Everyone* has many different selves, and the nature and balance of these selves gives us our own unique personality. Since we create our own reality, it is crucial that we know which of our many selves is in control!

When we are very young, our natural tendency is to be spontaneous, playful, open, happy, fearless, and full of wonder, and this Child within us never dies. Whether we are nine or ninety, the Free Child is still alive and is the source of our joy, spontaneity and sense of fun.

However, by the age of five or six, the Free Child has been displaced by the Wounded Child. By this time, we have realised — much to our surprise and dismay — that the world does not revolve around us. In order to have our parents' approval, it is not enough to simply be ourselves; we have to be *good*. Around this age, the Child decides that it is not loved enough. (However much we are loved, it is never good enough for the Child.) The Child wants perfect, unconditional love — and nothing less will do, and so it withdraws into its shell, and 'freezes' in time. This is the Wounded Child within us — unhappy, frightened, lost, angry and manipulative — still searching for unconditional love, still refusing to come out and play until it receives that love.

Time is an illusion. The Child within does not know that you are 'now' 30, 40 or 70 years old. For the Child, there is only the eternal present and, whatever your age, the Child will demand that its five-year-old needs are met. It is desperately seeking love and approval.

> *The Child does exist at this very moment as a living, breathing organism, and it has impact, tremendous impact, upon your reality. If you let that Child live your life, then you never do.*
>
> *(Lazaris)*[2]

Melanie's father was a foreign affairs correspondent, who spent much of his time abroad. He was a larger-than-life character who, on trips home to his wife and three daughters, would throw extravagant parties and invite a steady stream of visitors, spending little time alone with his family. His wife turned a blind eye to his numerous affairs, and devoted herself to charitable works. Melanie lived in awe of her father, who rarely even spoke to her — and her most fervent desire was to receive his love and attention.

When Melanie was sixteen, her father died of a heart attack and the Child within her embarked on a grim, resolute search for love. For several years, Melanie slept with any man who showed a vague interest in her. Most were insensitive, extrovert philanderers who merely wanted a brief affair — and as each man walked out on her, the Child within grew more and more desperate. Her task seemed more and more hopeless, and she became deeply depressed.

The problem was that Melanie was allowing the Child to run her adult life. The Child within simply wants to replay the past, 'undoing' what went wrong by getting it right *this* time around. The Child cannot make adult choices. Melanie's Child repeatedly chose men who were like her father — men with whom she had little hope of finding love — because it was still trying to re-play her childhood, in hope of a happy ending.

In therapy, Melanie found that there was another solution. Instead of allowing the Child to 'act out' in her *adult* life, she could give the Child what it wanted in its *own* reality, leaving her free to get on with her life. In meditation, she met the Child within, frozen in time at the age of five. The Child was sitting alone at the top of the staircase, listening to the raised voices and laughter of a party downstairs, and hugging the banister. The Adult Melanie sat down beside her, explaining that she was Melanie, twenty years on, and that she had come to be her Child's friend. Then she listened to the Child as it told her of its frustrations, fears and longings — and she held it in her arms, rocking it to sleep.

In the weeks that followed, Melanie learnt to give *herself* what she had been searching for from other people. In meditation, she gave her Child all of the unconditional love that it craved. Whatever the Child wanted, she provided — not in her adult reality, but in the *Child's* reality. She took it to a funfair, and bought it candy floss. She read it a bedtime story. It asked for a giant teddy bear, so she gift-wrapped one and tied it with a red bow for her delighted Child. And — most powerful of all — when her Child wept over her father ignoring her, Melanie visualised her father hugging the Child, and taking it on a sightseeing trip, with the Child beaming and rosy-cheeked with excitement.

As she grew to love the Child within, Melanie found that her own personality began to change. She became more self-confident, more fun-loving, more spontaneous. She discovered a great love for nature, and went on long country walks; and she abandoned the fleeting affairs which had caused her so much pain,

Coming to know and love the Child within is not simply a lighthearted way of passing the odd half-hour. It is an immensely powerful way of changing our lives. The Child will simply recreate the past over and over again. It is trying to 'perfect' our childhood, to 'get it right' this time. It is incapable of looking to the future. It is a victim of the past. Whatever the costs, it will seek love and approval — often in the most unlikely places, and in the most unlikely ways — and will not learn from its mistakes. But if we *give* that inner Child the love it hungers for, in its *own* reality, then it will no longer need to express itself in our adult world. By 'visiting' the Child within for just fifteen minutes each week, and honouring its needs, we can transform our lives.

As the Wounded Child is healed, we release the free Child within — and with it, our spontaneity, laughter, joy, love, and sense of wonder. If we have not recaptured the delights of the free Child, we are barely half-alive.

THE INNER CHILD

Relax deeply, then imagine yourself in the place you lived in when you were four to six years old. (If you lived in two or more houses during that period, trust your subconscious mind to pick and choose.) Walk around the house, seeing the familiar rooms and furniture, using all your senses to find yourself back there. Then, when you are ready, start to look for your Child — perhaps in the bedroom, perhaps the living room, perhaps in the garden. Your Child will be there somewhere, all alone.

When you find your Child, introduce yourself, and say you have come to be its friend. Then spend time regularly with your Child, getting to know it, listening to it, loving it. Provide it with an imaginary safe place, a sanctuary, which it can visit at any time. Whatever your Child wants, give it — in meditation. Most of all, offer your Child unconditional love — warmth, hugs, attention, respect, caring, intimacy. Watch the Child being transformed by your love — and loving in return.

When Lorraine first met her inner Child, she found that, although the Child smiled sweetly and listened politely, it would not speak. She assumed that she was not yet able to 'hear' it, and visited the Child several times more. Eventually, she asked the Child why it was so quiet. 'Children should be seen and not heard' it softly replied. Lorraine suddenly realised why she had always been so afraid of being noticed.

She had been the unexpected child of a menopausal mother. Her father had already retired when she was born, and wanted a quiet life, so Lorraine's mother would repeatedly tell her 'Shush! You'll disturb your father!' If she was playful or exuberant, she would be smacked for being noisy. She soon learnt that it was wiser to be silent.

Lorraine grew up to be painfully shy, and was unable to make friends or advance in her career. She was afraid of having any impact upon other people because her Child 'knew' that being noticed meant censure and disapproval. Through her inner journey Lorraine was able to lovingly encourage her Child to laugh and play and shout — and as her Child gained confidence, so did she.

Jenny's Child was also afraid of being visible, but for

different reasons. Jenny grew up in what she described as 'a happy, loving family', in which the children were often put first. However, her parents both felt thwarted in their own ambitions, and expected their children to fulfil their own needs. By the age of six, Jenny knew that her sole purpose in life was to make her parents proud of her. If she came top in class, her parents would celebrate; if she came second, they would patiently grill her on why she had 'failed'. Playing with friends was viewed as wasting precious time. Jenny's childhood was devoted to trying to be 'perfect' for her parents — regardless of her own needs and desires. Almost inevitably, Jenny's inner Child was scared of being noticed — whatever she said or did, it was never quite 'perfect' enough.

In meditation, Jenny was able to re-play various scenes from her childhood, in which the adult Jenny played the part of her Child's parent and would express delight at the young Jenny for having fun, coming third or fourth in a class test, or doing whatever she wished to do. As her Child was released, so Jenny began to feel free to be herself, rather than being 'perfect'.

Some people strongly resist feeling any love for the Child within. Richard was a self-employed accountant, who worked at least seventy hours a week — not because he needed the money, or enjoyed the work, but because he felt quite unable to relax. As a result, his marriage had ended in divorce. His father had been bad-tempered and sometimes violent, and Richard remembered his childhood as lonely and unhappy. His parents had run a highly successful retail business, and the Child within him was still trying to gain their love and approval, by being a workaholic.

When Richard visited his Child in meditation, he found it sitting in the middle of a large, empty room with bare floorboards. The Child was filthy and unkempt, smeared with faeces, and staring into space. When I encouraged the adult Richard to approach, he refused to do so, saying the Child disgusted him. For several months, he insisted that his Child was quite unlovable, and would not even speak to it. In the meantime, he worked longer and longer hours — until one evening he broke down in tears at his desk, weeping with confusion and exhaustion. His Child was wrecking his adult life.

Gradually, Richard realised that his refusal to take care of his Child was due to Ego payoffs. Firstly, he was unwilling to let go of his anger towards his parents. He wished to carry on blaming them for his problems, and refusing to take responsibility for his own life. Secondly, he believed that his puritan work ethic made him 'better than' other people. Thirdly, he was afraid of intimacy, and despite his claim that he wanted a close relationship, and regretted the breakdown of his marriage, his working hours safely precluded getting close to anyone. No wonder he was so reluctant to comfort his inner Child, and no wonder his poor Child was kicking up such a fuss.

Whatever our Child believes, we *were* loved 'enough' — since if we are not given enough love, we either die or become institutionalised. A famous study[3] of infants in a children's home in the 1940s, who were fed, clothed and kept warm but, due to pressures on staff, were not held, cuddled and spoken to, showed that the infants failed to thrive. Some simply withered away and died. If you are reading this, you had 'enough' love. The rest is up to you.

FAIRY TALES

What were your favourite fairy tales or storybooks when you were a child? Which stories did you read again and again? Take a fresh look at them. What were the subtle (and not-so-subtle) messages those tales gave you about life? For example, Cinderella: 'Wait for your Prince(ss) to come and rescue you.' 'Suffering is always rewarded in the end.' Sleeping Beauty: 'Life does not begin until your Prince(ss) has arrived.' 'If you're good, someone bad will be out to get you.' Red Riding Hood: 'The world is a dangerous place.' 'Don't trust other people.' And so on.

   Have any of these messages affected your attitude towards adult life? Do you still need to change these beliefs? What are your Negative Ego payoffs in hanging on to these fairy-tale beliefs and attitudes?

Just a few years after the Child freezes in time, we are faced with the crisis of puberty and suddenly the body becomes a strange, alien force quite beyond our control. With the arrival of emotional and bodily changes, the child catches a glimpse of approaching adulthood — and it panics. For a while, it may become clingy and dependent again, in an attempt to turn back the clock — but then comes the harsh realisation: growing up is inevitable! At this point — usually between the ages of twelve and fourteen — the inner Adolescent becomes crystallised.

The Adolescent has a dull, arid picture of what adulthood is all about. It sees adults as sensible, rational, boring, practical, and weighed down with responsibilities. To the Adolescent, the end of childhood represents an end to fun, freedom, spontaneity, laughter and joy. No wonder it is reluctant to grow up!

The Adolescent fantasy is that its unrecognised genius, talent or beauty will one day be discovered. Without any effort on its part, of course. The Adolescent within — full of Ego and martyr — dreams of winning the Pools, but never bothers to enter. It fantasises about visiting Katmandu, but never collects the travel brochures. It waits for a famous director to turn up on the doorstep offering a starring role in the latest blockbuster, when it hasn't even attended drama college. It lives in a world of fantasy.

Just as the Child is forever yearning for love, the Adolescent seeks firstly, to be in total control, and secondly, to be perfectly understood without having to explain itself. Its bargain is that it will grow up *only* if life is just as it wants it to be. Otherwise, no deal! Many people live out their lives waiting for this guarantee to be met. In the meantime — despite outward appearances — they refuse to become adults.

Sheila had a problem with compulsive shoplifting. Several times a week, she would find herself wandering around shops in a daze, stuffing fancy goods and jewellery into her bag, making no attempt to conceal her crime. She had been sent to prison twice. In therapy, she spoke to her Shoplifting Self (using the 'empty chair' technique) and, to her surprise, found an angry Adolescent, who felt fully justified in what she was doing: 'Why *shouldn't* I have nice things? No-one has ever been nice to me!' But as soon as Sheila replied to the girl, suggesting that she was creating even more problems for herself, a second child came to occupy the empty chair — a little girl who was plagued with guilt. This Child felt that she must have done something to *deserve* her unhappy childhood; she wanted to get caught for shoplifting, so that she would be punished for being so wicked. Between them, the two girls were wrecking Sheila's adult life.

Fortunately — just as the Wounded Child can give way to the Free Child — hidden beneath the fears and fantasies of the Adapted Adolescent is its positive counterpart, the Curious Adolescent: exploring, questioning, wondering, inquisitive, inventive, imaginative, enthusiastic, creative and visionary. By befriending the Adolescent within, we can release this endless source of creativity and wonder.

THE ADOLESCENT

It is now time to meet your Adolescent. Picture yourself in the house where you lived when you were twelve to fourteen years old. (Trust your subconscious to know how old your Adolescent is.) Use all your senses to find yourself there. Then look around the house until you find your Adolescent, all alone.

As with your Child, introduce yourself to the Adolescent — and start becoming acquainted. Get to know its hopes, fears and fantasies. Try to understand how it sees the world. Give it whatever it wants — within your inner reality — and express your love, warmth and tenderness.

Sam was in his mid-thirties, but his attitudes revealed that he was just an overgrown adolescent at heart. After leaving home at sixteen — 'My parents were impossible' — he had switched from one job to another, rarely settling for more than six months at a time. He had yet to decide upon a career. His relationships, similarly, had been brief and superficial, and he expressed horror at the thought of making any commitment. As soon as there was a problem, he simply packed his bags and left.

For Sam, everything was black and white — good or bad, right or wrong, brilliant or idiotic. There was no room for debate, no allowance for complexity, no possibility of his being wrong. Like a teenager, he was always playing to the crowd, always trying to impress. Everything was done for show, or in an attempt to shock, rather than from any genuine desire. But under his bluff exterior, Sam was lonely, miserable and frightened. His Adolescent was in control of his life.

As soon as there is a whiff of responsibility in the air, the fearful Adolescent sprints in the opposite direction. It consistently blames others for its predicaments — particularly parents and other authority figures. While our Adolescent is playing 'If it weren't for you' (one of its favourite games) we remain trapped by our past.

Josie, whose mother walked out on her when she was seven, yelled at me 'I will *never* forgive her — never, ever!' Yet by clinging to her anger and resentment, she was condemning herself to recreate the past, sabotaging her life at every turn to 'prove' how much her mother had messed her up.

I suggested that Josie might write her mother's life story — from the point of view of a sympathetic, loving friend — up to the time when her mother decided to leave her husband and children. Josie felt unable to do this for several months, but eventually tackled the project. Amidst flowing tears, she wrote about her mother entering a loveless marriage at the age of sixteen, in order to escape an unhappy childhood, then feeling trapped and suffocated by the demands of three children and an unsupportive husband. Her mother had not had any chance to grow up herself. For the first time, Josie began to realise how desperately unhappy her mother must have been in order to desert her family — and forgiveness at last became a possibility.

By forgiving those who have harmed us in the past, we free *ourselves*. If we are concerned with injustices 'done to us', we attract more of the same experiences. We do not need to *love* those who have mistreated us, but for our own sake, we need to forgive them. According to *A Course In Miracles* 'Forgiveness is the key to happiness.'[4] By forgiving others — from our heart, not our mind — we release ourselves from the past. 'The more you hate something, the more you are bound to it,' says Orin[5] 'and the more you love it the freer you are. So as you love your past, you are free from it.' All that stands in the way is our old payoffs — our self-righteousness, our self-pity, our need to 'punish', avoiding responsibility, clinging to the past.

After all, we *choose* our parents — so blaming them for how we were treated is like selecting a bowl of green apples, and then complaining that what we *really* wanted was a dish of strawberries. Whatever the challenges and stresses of our childhood, we carefully chose our parents in the hope that we would learn and grow from the experience — and they agreed to 'play the game' with us, and allow us to be *their* teachers. Once we take responsibility for our choices, and recognise the lessons we hoped to learn, there is nothing to forgive. We are never at the mercy of our childhood. It influences, but does not control us. We are not helpless puppets. We only accept those hang-ups from the past which suit us.

One of my clients, who longed to break down and cry, told me that his parents had brought him up to believe it was shameful for a man to cry — in public or in private — and implied that he was a helpless victim of that belief. I said, as gently as I could, that he had probably been told as a child that the moon was made of cheese, but at some stage he had revised that belief. If a six-year-old child has the power to change its beliefs, then so has a forty-year-old man! Our beliefs, as Seth says, are just like children's playing blocks. They are only glued in position by our fears, payoffs and hidden agendas.

LOOKING AT CHILDHOOD

1) Write down the worst aspects of your childhood. What are the circumstances, situations, events or parental attitudes and characteristics that you would most like to have changed? What did you resent most about your childhood? Or about your parents? Now look at your list, and think about what you *gained* from those difficulties. Looking back, what lessons did you learn? What emotional strengths and qualities did you acquire? What helpful decisions did you make as a result of those experiences? Why might you have chosen your parents? What did you learn from them?

2) What messages did your family give you about adult life? Do any of the following sound familiar?
* Work hard and play hard.
* Schooldays are the best days of your life.
* Don't let us down.
* Always put others first.
* Spare the rod and spoil the child.
* Be good.

* A job worth doing is worth doing well.
* What will the neighbours think?
* Hear no evil, speak no evil, see no evil.
* When the going gets tough, the tough get going.
* Find a nice man/woman to take care of you.
* Always put on a smile.
* The only person you can rely on is yourself.
* Life is hard for people like us/you.
* Just get a steady job with a pension.

Think about the spoken and unspoken messages you received about adulthood when you were a child. How have these messages influenced your life? Do you need to reassess any of these beliefs and attitudes?

The stiffest tree is readiest for the axe.
The strong and mighty topple from their place;
The soft and yielding rise above them all.

(Tao Te Ching)[6]

Lazaris suggests[7] that, between the ages of eighteen and twenty-one, another sub-personality is born — the Young Adult. This is where millions of us get stuck. Although we might be outwardly successful in life, our personal growth ended abruptly all those years ago. The Young Adult can give a convincing impression of being an Adult, and might go unrecognised for a whole lifetime. However, there are several characteristics which give it away:

Firstly, the Young Adult is rigid and inflexible. It *knows* it is right, and sees little point in discussion — although it will gladly show you the error of your ways. Whereas the Adolescent is vehement and rebellious in its views, the Young Adult is calm and patronising in the face of opposition.

Pompous politicians who boast of not having changed their views in twenty years, or never being 'swayed' by others' opinions, are good examples of the Young Adult in action. Whether radical or conservative in its outlook, the Young Adult prides itself on its ability to 'stand firm', and ignore others' viewpoints. Like the Adolescent, the Young Adult is black-and-white in its way of seeing, favours simplistic solutions, and avoids the real issues.

The Young Adult skates across the surface of life, with rigid opinions, beliefs and goals, unable to grow and develop in the here-and-now, scared of closeness and intimacy, emotionally numb. It has revamped the Adolescent's fantasies, and taken them as its own. But it does not want to *realise* those fantasies. No, it just enjoys *pretending* that it wants them — and then luxuriating in the self-pity and better-thans that arise from being 'prevented' from doing so. According to the Young Adult, the world 'owes' it.

Young Adults will often be busy-busy, fluttering about from one activity to the next. They are *much* too busy and important to waste a moment — and might be very scathing about those who have time to stand and stare. However, their achievements feel shallow, meaningless and unsatisfying.

There is no point in trying to negotiate with the Young Adult within us. It is much too arrogant, dogmatic and inflexible. It is much too puffed up with Negative Ego. However, by *listening* to our Young Adult, we can begin to recognise and transcend it.

THE YOUNG ADULT

Imagine yourself in a summer meadow, sitting amidst long grass and wild flowers, looking upon a blue lake which sparkles in the sunlight. Take a few minutes to find yourself in this beautiful place.

Then turn away from the lake, and search for a well which leads deep into the earth. There will be a ladder or rope, so that you can climb down into it. Clamber into the well, touching the soft, crumbling walls, smelling the earth, hearing your footsteps echo as you move deeper and deeper underground.

Eventually the well opens up into a bare, dimly-lit cavern. Walk into the cavern, and look around you. In the middle, there is a rather grand chair — and there, all alone, sits your Young Adult.

Approach your Young Adult, and ask it to tell you all about itself. Gather as much information as you can about its beliefs, attitudes, values and fantasies, so that you will recognise it when it pops up in your adult reality. Then ask it to join you in the light, and retrace your steps.

As you both emerge from the well, the summer landscape fills you with its light and beauty. Walk towards the lake and immerse yourselves in the cool sparkling water — seeing your Young Adult become radiant with light. Then gently come back to the room.

> *The attainment of autonomy is manifested by the*
> *release or recovery of three capacities: awareness,*
> *spontaneity and intimacy.*
>
> *(Eric Berne)*[8]

According to Lazaris, unless someone has made a conscious decision to be an Adult — not just saying the words, but *deciding* to live as an Adult — then they are still an Adolescent or Young Adult. And if you are not an Adult, then spiritual growth is quite impossible. If you are not an Adult then, however 'successful' you might be, this will be a wasted lifetime.

So how can we tell the difference between a *real* grown-up — an Adult — and a Young Adult which is disguising itself as an adult?

* Adults enthusiastically take responsibility for their own life. They never blame their childhood, or other people.

* Adults are flexible and fluid. They have clarified their own values, principles, ideals and goals, but all of these are open to scrutiny and change — and none are imposed upon other people.

* Adults have their own Dreams, which they are actively moving towards — and they enjoy the *process* of doing so.

* Adults behave with honesty and integrity, listening to their inner self, and respecting others.

* Adults enjoy life — they have fun!

THE ADULT

Assess your own status as an Adult.
* Do you willingly take responsibility for your own life — whatever happens?
* Are you clear about your ideals, values, opinions, likes, dislikes and beliefs?
* Are these flexible and ever-changing?
* Do you resist trying to impose your views on others, or trying to 'impress'?
* Have you clarified your Dreams for the future?
* Are you *actively* creating your own future?
* How honest are you — with yourself and others?
* Are you respectful of yourself and others?
* Do you behave with integrity, whatever the situation?

If you cannot honestly answer Yes to all nine questions, what are your payoffs for refusing to be an Adult? What are the costs? Are you ready to make the decision to be an Adult from now on? If so, in what ways do you need to change?

Maria had an inner self which constantly threw doubt on everything she said, and warned her not to trust me because I would use it against her, and probably admit her to hospital. After several months, she blurted out that she could not be honest with me because of this carping, critical voice in her head, which had governed her life since she was six years old. She called it The Commentator. Naturally, The Commentator was furious that Maria had revealed her 'secret', and she allowed it to punish her for several weeks. However, now that we were able to *discuss* The Commentator, she slowly gained a new perspective on it. Instead of seeing it as proof that she was 'mad', and being terrified of it, she could see it as a normal part of her personality, one of her many inner selves. The only problem was that, believing it protected her, she had given it too much power. Gradually, Maria learnt to recognise its voice, and would occasionally repeat its comments to me during our sessions — much to its horror! She was then able to decide whether to take it seriously, or simply reassure it that she could take care of *herself*.

In transactional analysis terms, The Commentator would be called a Critical Parent figure. Critical Parent is the inner self which expresses all the negativity and criticism of our early experiences. It is the self which reinforces our Child's belief that it is unloved and unlovable. It tut-tuts, reproaches, reprimands, scolds, punishes, castigates, lectures, belittles, judges and condemns. It is the voice of disapproval, of censure — directed at ourselves and/ or other people. It favours words such as 'should', 'must' and 'ought.' It is saturated with Ego.

Fortunately, we have a Nurturing Parent figure too. Nurturing Parent represents all the warmth, love and support we were offered in childhood, whether from parents, relatives, neighbours, friends or teachers. Nurturing Parent encourages us to take care of ourselves and others — including our own children — and helps to release the Free Child.

Many people can track down a dozen or more different selves within. There might be Tantrum Timmy, Soft Touch, Wide Eyes, Earth Mother, Moaning Minnie, Dithering Dick, The Chatterbox, The Wise Owl, Poor Me, The Dreamer, Stuff Shirt, Little Cutie, The Dictator, Slowcoach, The Puritan, Life's Too Short, Pig Parent, The

Angel, Cop-Out Charlie, The Worrier, Little Professor, Blurt-It-Out, The Saboteur, Fun Lover, Prim And Proper, Brave Bertie, The Mule, Pull Your Socks Up, The Charmer, Rave It Up, Can't Cope, Hurry Along — and so on. Every time our 'mood' changes, we have slipped into a different self.

By learning to recognise the various aspects of our personality — through *experiencing* them — and knowing the beliefs, payoffs and hidden agendas of each, we can avoid being controlled by them. For example, if we are jealous because our partner has just seen an old flame, we might feel overwhelmed with that emotion. But if we can say 'This is just Old Green Eyes throwing a wobbler again' then we gain some perspective on the situation.

If your head is spinning at the thought of ten or twenty different people bustling around inside your head, vying with each other as to whose beliefs and payoffs will win out, don't worry! All of these selves can be categorised as either Child, Adolescent or Parent, and many people simply work with their inner Child, recognise their Ego payoffs and ignore the rest of their inner community!

The good news is that *everyone* has the liberating, creative, joyful and loving selves within. We have everything we need to create a life full of love, peace, joy and fulfilment. Each of us has a Free Child, a Curious Adolescent and a Nurturing Parent — however much we try to suppress them. And the synergy of these (plus a Supportive Ego) — the whole which is greater than the sum of its parts — is the Adult.

YOUR INNER SELVES

During the next few days, do several spot-checks on which of your sub-personalities come to the surface in various situations. Learn to distinguish their different voices, comments and turns of phrase, and learn to love and accept them all.

Look out for the Wounded Child — hurt, approval-seeking, manipulative, confused and frightened; the Free Child — fun-loving and spontaneous; the Adolescent — panicky, perfectionistic and trying to impress, or curious and creative; the Young Adult — rigid, patronising, and emotionally numb; the Critical Parent, and the Nurturing Parent; and the mature, integrated Adult. Which sub-personalities are in control of your life? Which are weak or absent? Which selves do you wish to cultivate and develop?

The shadowy figures from the past are precisely what you must escape. They are not real, and have no hold over you unless you bring them with you ... For the past can cast no shadow to darken the present, unless you are afraid of the light.

(A Course In Miracles)[9]

Our current, linear concept of time leads us to believe that we have a fixed, immutable past. We feel convinced that the past is Real, that it cannot be changed, that it is stable and permanent. But metaphysics argues that we have many, many probable pasts. We can pick and choose!

Indeed, we do this all the time. We continually re-write the past, as we recall some memories and suppress others, or even unwittingly create new memories, according to our changing beliefs. As Seth suggests, we are not at the mercy of our past because we are constantly creating that past.

If memories of childhood are disturbing our adult life, then we can *change* those memories. Our memories are based upon our beliefs. If we believe that we had a desperately unhappy childhood, or a wicked stepmother, or that we were ceaselessly teased at school, then we will selectively remember events which confirm and support those beliefs. (Unfortunately, psychotherapy often serves to reinforce negative beliefs, through focusing on the traumas of the past.)

If we are allowing our negative beliefs to interfere with life, then we have payoffs and hidden agendas for doing so — perhaps a need to punish, clinging to self-pity, avoidance of responsibility, or an excuse for failure. But as we let go of the payoffs, we can release the old batch of memories and select new memories — memories of happy times in childhood, of stepmother being kind and caring, of having fun at school. (Yes, those memories will be tucked away somewhere!) It is the same childhood, but a different set of memories.

To take an analogy, if you used to perceive your childhood as looking like a duck — as in the famous duck-rabbit figure on page 207 — then now it appears like a rabbit. You can still 'see' the duck if you choose, but now that you have seen the rabbit, it will never be the same again.

If we wish, we can even scribble out the duck-rabbit, and draw a squirrel instead! If some aspects of the past feel so disturbing that we wish they had never happened, then we can 'edit out' those events from the film-like illusion we call

our 'past'. We can simply snip out that section of the film. After all, reality is an illusion that *we* create. All we need to do is re-play that period several times in our imagination — vividly and with great emotion and desire — *without* the trauma; and 'remember' the different future that followed. Seth states[10] that this is not a form of self-deception, but an actual re-creation of the past, a choice of a different 'probable past' — and by changing the past in our mind, we also change our present and future. We shift into a different 'probable reality'. (If you feel resistance to letting go of the past so easily, then your payoffs might be keeping you stuck. Or perhaps you learnt important lessons from those experiences, which you do not wish to forget.)

If this seems hard to swallow, then you can change the past in more symbolic ways. In meditation, you can *become* the loving parent which your Child needed in the past. Or, if memories of your parents' constant squabbling are reinforcing a belief that marriage never works, you can visualise them being caring, respectful and affectionate with one another. If the future of our Dreams seems inconsistent with our past, then we can change the past! We have the power to invent new 'memories' for ourselves, which accord with our new beliefs. Present unhappiness is never 'caused' by the past; but it might result from how we choose to see the past, *right now*.

> *As you change your past in your mind, you change your vibration and begin to draw to yourself a new future ... It doesn't matter if this was your 'real' past; your subconscious mind doesn't know the difference. It will draw circumstances to you that match your imagined past.*
>
> *(Orin)*[11]

RELEASING THE PAST

1) What do you tell yourself or other people about your childhood? What negative beliefs do you hold about your childhood and adolescence — about your relationship with your parents, brothers and sisters, or your experience at school, or your friends, or the effects of your family circumstances?

Write down the reverse of each belief — e.g. 'My stepmother adored me', 'I had a wonderful time at school' — and search your past for memories which support those positive beliefs. Or simply invent a new past for yourself. If you feel resistance to doing this, or your mind goes blank, examine your payoffs for clinging to the old beliefs.

2) Think about two or three difficult, traumatic or lonely periods in the past when you really needed love, support and friendship — times you still think of occasionally, times which still seem emotionally

charged. Then, in meditation, visit those 'earlier'
selves — and give them love, strength, courage and
hope. You might wish to picture them surrounded
with white light; or to introduce yourself as their
future self, and give them hugs and encouragement;
or to 'rewind the film', and write a new scene into
your past.

Channelled sources suggest that the future is now becoming more and more influential in our lives. The inner Child
and Adolescent will remain as active as ever in the New
Age, but 'the backdrop of the past' will seem more and more
flimsy. It is now becoming less credible to see the present
as the mere effect, the fallout, of the past. Lazaris notes[12]
that even our physical body — from our frontal lobes and
ventricles to our endocrine glands and immune system — is
oriented towards the *future*, towards the possibilities and
probabilities that lie ahead. Our present is motivated by
what we are becoming.

What is more, we are responsible not only for our
personal future, but for the *global* future which we are
helping to create. It has never been so crucial to leave
behind the shadowlands of the past, to release our Child
and Adolescent from their timeless torment — and to begin
to Dream of the future.

8
Awakening to Your Dream

All the world's a stage,
And all the men and women merely players,
They have their exits and their entrances,
And one man in his time plays many parts...
(As You Like It)[1]

Over the centuries, many — like Shakespeare — have compared our lives with self-contained plays or novels: each with its own themes, plots, sub-plots, major and minor characters, and walk-on parts. This is not just an intriguing idea, a metaphor, but is quite *literally* true. Life is just an illusion. The world is a giant theatre. We are all so utterly absorbed, so totally convincing in our roles, that even *we* forget we are just acting, that it is just a stage set. We believe that it is Real!

What is more, everyone writes, produces, directs and stars in their own production. Some might choose a tragic script, perhaps Hamlet or Anna Karenina, while others select a romantic comedy such as A Midsummer Night's Dream, or a visionary quest such as the Search for the Holy Grail. But if we don't like our script, we can change it. Neither fate nor God chose our script — *we* did — and if it is tragic, painful, or simply dull and mediocre, we can decide to re-write it. Day by day, moment by moment, we create our own reality.

So why do we pick one script rather than another? Because as spiritual beings, we wish to learn and grow. At a higher level of consciousness — before we entered this lifetime — we chose to work on certain themes, to overcome given blockages and limitations, to develop certain personal qualities and to make our unique contribution to society. Then we carefully selected our culture, background, race, sex, parents and childhood experiences to match our intended life-themes. By examining our past, the challenges we have faced, our skills and interests, our sources of joy, we can unearth the recurring themes, focuses, tasks or goals we decided upon before we were born — and, since the present moment is always our point of power, we can switch to other aims if we wish.

Our life-themes will, naturally, require personal and spiritual growth: coming to know ourselves, learning to love, realising our connectedness with others, overcoming blockages and limitations, expressing our potential and strengths, transcending the Ego, becoming whole, being creative, being joyful.

According to Lazaris, two life focuses are mandatory for all of us: firstly, *learning* how to have fun, and secondly, *consciously* creating success. This means continually redefining for ourselves what we mean by 'fun' and 'success', and learning how to create those experiences in our lives — by processing our negative beliefs, payoffs and hidden agendas, and programming what we want. In addition, Lazaris suggests[2] we have chosen five individual focuses — making the 'magic number' seven in all.

LIFE-THEME: LOVE
Many of us choose to explore the many sides of *love*— through love for friends, lovers, children, family, pets, or perhaps through our love for the countryside, animals, art, music, a hobby or pursuit, the planet or God.

Pauline was born into a family which was riddled with

sexual abuse. She was abused by her father, two uncles and brother throughout her childhood and—like so many abused women — grew up hating and blaming herself. It was less frightening, as a child, to imagine that she somehow 'deserved' her suffering (and therefore could *stop* it, if only she could work out what she was doing wrong), than to conclude that her parents were 'bad' or incapable of loving (which would have meant there was no hope that the abuse might end). Since Pauline felt she deserved abuse, and believed that all men were the same, she later married a man who was also physically and sexually abusive. Even her friends took advantage of her. For Pauline, 'love' meant hurt, pain and suffering.

Eventually, through joining an incest survivors' group, Pauline began to release her hurt and anger, and deal with her low self-esteem. She realised that unless she changed *now,* her childhood abuse would wreck her adulthood; she would be an incest victim for the rest of her life. Instead of constantly reliving her tragic childhood, and blaming herself or her family, she gradually began to live in the present, and look towards the future. She became determined that even if no-one else ever loved her, she would learn to love herself. She had discovered one of her life focuses. As Pauline slowly began to love and respect herself, so the pattern of her relationships changed.

Does this mean that she *wanted* to be abused as a child, that she *chose* to be abused? Of course not. But *at a higher level,* she did choose her parents and — like so many others in her generation — perhaps she knew she would have the strength and love to *break* the 'chain of abuse' which trailed back through many generations, and would thus prevent others suffering.

Not everyone who chooses love as a life-theme will give

themselves such a traumatic and challenging start in life. However, we will often set up blockages of one kind or another.

Charlie grew up with a boundless love for literature. From the age of seven, he recalls spending every spare moment in the local library, poring over mythology and the classics. The problem was that his father, who worked down the pits, was illiterate, and regarded reading as 'cissy'. He refused to allow books into the house, so Charlie learnt never to speak of his secret passion. When he later begged to go to university, his father refused and Charlie, caught between his love for his family, and his love for books, reluctantly became a miner. It was nearly ten years before he broke free from his family, pursued his first love, and started a rewarding career as an English teacher. Some time later, he 'happened' to overhear his father speaking proudly of his 'clever son'.

LIFE-THEME: EMOTIONS

Both Pauline and Charlie had probably also chosen to handle specific *emotions* in this lifetime. Learning to express and release one or more emotions which we frequently block or deny — 'positive' emotions such as happiness, joy, delight and enthusiasm, as well as the 'negative' emotions such as anger, hurt, guilt and fear — is another common life focus.

Focusing on emotions will usually mean that we repeatedly invite situations — scenes within our overall play — which give us the opportunity to experience and deal with those feelings. If you wish to learn about guilt, for example, then you will create excuses to feel guilty by choosing manipulative friends and relatives, or by breaking rules — so that you can convert your guilt into resentment, and release it.

If you have difficult relationships — past or present — then ask yourself which emotions those relationships rouse in you. It is quite likely that you wished to explore these feelings in this lifetime. The people involved are just willing actors in your play.

LIFE-THEME: EGO

Others choose their *Ego* as a focus, perhaps wishing to deal with their self-pity, martyrdom, arrogance or abuse of power. In this case, your family background or childhood experiences will probably have encouraged you to feel 'better than' or 'less than' other people, so that you are faced with the challenge of overcoming that early conditioning. Perhaps you will have chosen privileged parents, or outstanding talent or intelligence, or a deprived start in life, or physical disability. Or you might have selected a society or family ridden by racial or religious 'better thans' — 'Whites are better than blacks', 'Catholics are better than Protestants', 'Gentiles are better than Jews', and so on — so that you are constantly assaulted with such prejudices. Or you might choose to rise to a powerful position — perhaps as a manager, judge, company director, doctor, journalist, politician, or simply as a parent — so that you can learn to use power wisely.

Lazaris often speaks of the difference between 'dominion' and 'domination', and urges us to move towards the power of dominion in our lives. Domination is the power of the Old Age — the power of oppression, control and manipulation, the power of inequality and injustice, the power of strength or weakness. When we try to dominate, we see the world as a scary, threatening place in which we must control or be controlled. We might struggle to reach the top, clambering over other people, convinced that there is not enough to go round, that Nature is cruel, that the 'nice guy or gal' always finishes last. Through fear, we might use the false power of threats and intimidation. Or, more commonly, we might strive to make people (or God) feel sorry for us — 'Look how I suffer!' — and blame others, in hope of being rescued from our self-imposed struggles. Either way, as bully or as victim, we are using the power of domination.

The power of dominion — the power of the New Age — involves assuming that the world is friendly, abundant and supportive, and willingly taking responsibility for our own lives. It means seeing power as the ability to *act*, rather than as power over others. It means actively and joyously reaching towards our future. It means 'co-creating' with God/dess, rather than manipulatively asking God/dess to take pity on us. The power of dominion is the power of love.

LIFE-THEME: 'MATRIX'

A related life-theme — apparently chosen by the majority of women alive today — is what Lazaris calls the *matrix*. The challenge of the femininity matrix is how to reconcile being *powerful* and *successful* with being feminine; that is, how to become one's *own* role model for a new, expansive vision of womanhood — a vision which goes beyond the old passive-dependent-nurturing feminine stereotype, and which rejects the idea that a 'successful' woman must think and act (and even dress) like a man, or strive for male ideals.

Like many women, I was strongly conditioned with 'Let the boy win at tennis' mentality, and grew up feeling highly ambivalent about success. There was always a dual message: 'Do your best! Be successful!' and, more subtly, 'But don't be *too* bright or successful, or you'll die a lonely old maid.' (It rarely occurred to me that a woman might *choose* — shock! horror! — to live without a man, or could reject men who wished her to play dumb or be an unpaid servant.) A woman's role in life was to totter two steps behind in the shadow of her husband, with children pulling at her skirt. In order to achieve success of any kind, she had to gain permission from men. Alternatively, she could be a 'career woman', and sacrifice her personal life — but it was an either-or choice. (More recently, an equally oppressive 'Superwoman' stereotype has emerged.)

The challenge for women today is to reject all this nonsense, and to reclaim our power: to ignore *men's* definitions of femininity, of success, of power, and to construct our *own* life-enhancing images of all three, as individual women. Then to become living embodiments of the Goddess within — to be feminine *and* powerful *and* successful.

Many men have chosen a similar life-theme: how to redefine power, success and masculinity in their own terms. More and more men are rejecting the tough, macho image of manhood, with its chauvinistic attitudes and the pressures of the rat-race. Instead, they are embracing love, warmth and tenderness, and the joys of fatherhood; they are searching for new meaning and understanding of what it is to be a man. Such men are weary of being told that 'big boys don't cry' and 'real men don't eat quiche', and wish to decide for themselves what to eat, wear, think, feel and desire — without being forced to relinquish their 'masculine' energy. For these men, the masculinity matrix will be a crucial life-theme.

THE MATRIX

Consider what you mean by being 'powerful', and being 'successful' — making these definitions entirely personal and positive. Avoid any negative concepts of power, such as being ruthless and materialistic, or climbing up the corporate ladder at the expense of one's personal life. Ignore others' ideas about what success 'should' mean to a man or woman. What would positive power and success mean to *you* in *your* life? What *action* might you take to move closer to these ideals?

LIFE-THEME: COMMUNICATION

Another common life-theme is *communication:* not gossip and small talk, but sharing ideas, concepts, philosophy, values, beliefs, attitudes and feelings. (If you loathe small talk, then communication is probably one of your themes.) Those who choose this focus often set up obstacles in their childhood; perhaps a family who constantly row, or confine their conversation to 'Pass the salt', or who believe that children should be seen and not heard; or perhaps a more physical blockage such as stammering, deafness or dyslexia.

In my own life, communication is a crucial theme, and one of my blockages was a fear of conflict. When I was a child, my family would chat quite merrily over the dinner table about what happened that day, our plans for the weekend, what friends and acquaintances were up to; but we never discussed literature, or politics, or social issues, or religion, or ethical dilemmas, or the meaning of life and death — not because we were unintelligent, but because we felt threatened by any difference of opinion or conflict. In our ever-happy family, there were never any arguments!

As a result, I grew up reluctant to challenge anyone, or to discuss difficult issues, since I assumed that conflict was dangerous. I had never learnt how to handle a disagreement, or resolve a conflict, other than by withdrawing or pretending to agree. My childhood solution to this dilemma was to express myself through short stories, songs, poems and diaries — and later magazine articles — since this indirect, one-sided form of communication avoided open conflict. I was in my mid-twenties before I began to express controversial views face-to-face, rather than from the relative 'safety' of my typewriter.

LIFE-THEME: TEACHING AND HEALING

Teaching and healing is another possible life focus, which might be expressed through being a schoolteacher, lecturer, nurse, therapist, homoeopath, spiritual healer, astrologer, social worker, priest, parent and so on. Of course, this does not mean that all nurses and doctors are healers, since many are not, nor that all teachers are succeeding in their life-purpose, since many believe that their sole function is to forcefeed with 'facts'; however, they do have the *opportunity* to be true teachers and healers through their work. Others will fulfil such a focus in less obvious ways — perhaps by being a shop assistant who always has a sunny smile and positive outlook, or a mother who teaches her children to love and respect themselves through her own example.

A Course In Miracles concludes with a 'teacher's manual', in the assumption that everyone is a teacher, whether formally or informally. It notes that all teaching is a process of learning, that teacher and pupil are One, and it emphasises that there are only two thought systems we can teach — that of the Ego, or that of the Self (or God/dess). Every time we meet someone, we might confirm their negativity, fear and doubt, or add to their love, light and joy — even if we are just buying a newspaper. Every day, we can leave people feeling weary, dispirited or fearful, or we can be sources of hope and inspiration.

LIFE-THEME: SERVING OTHERS

Serving others is also a common life purpose — whether this is expressed by serving individuals, society, or humanity as a whole. The 'helping professions' — nursing, medicine, counselling, psychotherapy, probation work, the ministry and so on — are an obvious means of reaching individuals in this way, as is voluntary and campaign work of various kinds. Working in the mass media can be a way of serving too — perhaps by exploring social problems, raising awareness, or challenging the status quo.

The danger in choosing to serve others is that we have to walk a tightrope. If we trip and fall to one side, we are swallowed up by our patronising, ever-superior Ego. ('Poor things! Those of us who are lucky enough to be healthy/ wealthy/wise should do our bit for them.' 'How wonderful I am to battle against this terrible oppression!') However, if we tumble over to the other side, we express another aspect of Ego: martyrhood. ('I try so hard, but it's all so frustrating and exhausting.') Either way, we are unlikely to truly 'help' a single soul. In order to avoid these traps, it is crucial to *receive* as much as we *give*.

LIFE-THEME: STRENGTHS

Many people choose to develop *personal qualities or strengths* as a life-theme — perhaps to learn forgiveness, or aesthetic appreciation, or creativity and productivity, or courage, or leadership, or wisdom, or faith, or responsibility, or compassion, or inner peace, or intellectual curiosity, or a sense of humour, or honesty and integrity, or the ability to make a commitment, or to consistently stand up for our principles, values and ideals. If so, we will create circumstances which provide us with appropriate challenges.

If you wish to learn forgiveness, for example, then naturally you will cast actors in your drama who will behave in a way that requires forgiveness — people who will abuse, betray, rob, despise or otherwise mistreat you or your loved ones. If you hope to develop honesty and integrity, then you will challenge yourself with situations in which it might be easier to lie, cheat or pretend.

Gary had chosen love, honesty and fighting injustice as three of his life focuses — and so he chose to be gay in this lifetime. This neatly gave him the opportunity to work towards all three goals — by being honest and 'coming out' to his friends and family, despite his fears of rejection, by forming a loving and committed relationship with his partner, and by getting involved in a campaign for gay rights.

For some, spirituality is a life focus — that is, consciously developing their relationship with God/dess, the Universe, All That Is or whichever term you prefer — perhaps through practising a religion of some kind, though not necessarily so. For such people, spiritual awareness imbues each and every moment of their lives with meaning and significance. It fills every situation with the potential for growth. It is an eternal source of love, light and joy.

Other life-themes might include converting weaknesses into strengths (for example, arrogance into self-confidence, self-deprecation into humility, greed into desire), learning to 'go with the flow', taking charge of your own life, trusting your inner wisdom, creating abundance, giving up being a doormat, or exploring the boundaries of consciousness.

Of course, we can and do work on themes which are not specific life focuses. Everyone will be faced with blockages and limitations, and hopefully we all aim to develop personal qualities and strengths. If we decide that love and honesty are not on our list of life-themes, this does not exempt us from being loving and honest! (And if we decide that it does, we might be setting up our life-themes for *next* time around!)

> *I am a fragment of reality*
> *struggling to know itself*
> *a talking partner fiercely thrown*
> *into the world to answer back*
> *and listen*
> *and act into some form*
> *the longing of what is in*
> *the possibility of being.*
>
> *(Miller Mair)*[3]

YOUR SCRIPT

Write your life story, as if it were an outline for a play or novel. Pick out the recurring themes, obstacles, triumphs and joys of the central character. What are the events in this script? What sort of roles appear? Why might someone have chosen this particular culture, background, family, strengths, weaknesses, abilities, interest and experiences? What challenges did they set up for themselves? What might they have hoped to learn or achieve? What would the best possible outcome be?

Look through the possible life-focuses listed above. Which of these make you tingle, or shift about uneasily, or sound like familiar themes in your life? Have you already achieved some of these goals? Which themes still need to be resolved? Which form an ongoing part of your life?

Would you like to change your focuses, and shift direction? If so, you are allowed to change your mind. The choice is always ours. If you are currently living out a mundane or painful script, you can switch to a magical script; after all, you're the scriptwriter!

YOUR LIFE'S WORK

Your dreams will come true as you follow your feelings of joy, delight and self-love.

(Orin)[4]

Channelled sources suggest that every one of us has a purpose, a mission, a unique role to play in the world — our life's work. Perhaps it will be based upon artistic or musical talent, or a love for children, or the ability to teach, or skill for organisation, or culinary flair, or affinity with nature, being a diplomat, or a mechanical wizard. Perhaps we are drawn towards a social, political or environmental cause of some kind. Or maybe we have an extraordinary passion for china dolls or medieval poetry. Each of us has a gift to give to the world — the gift of our own uniqueness.

Whatever our life purpose, it will involve making some contribution to people, other living beings, or the planet, and once we discover our life's work, the doors to joy and abundance will swing wide open. If you suffer from Monday morning blues, or watch the clock all day, or envy people who bounce out of bed in eager anticipation of the tasks ahead, then you are not doing your life's work — and you might be well advised to start searching for it.

The clue lies in your enthusiasm — the God/dess within — what you most love to do. If you work as a librarian, but can scarcely wait to arrive home and play your saxophone, then perhaps your future lies in music? If you earn your living as a secretary, but your greatest joy is in caring for your dogs, then perhaps your true vocation lies in working with animals? If you work as a housewife, and enjoy balancing the budget, then perhaps you would thrive on setting up your own business, or fund-raising for charity?

Many of us share the Old Age belief that work has to be unpleasant or restrictive — that we have to suffer to earn our daily crust, or that we 'should' be satisfied with humdrum routine, joylessness and mediocrity. While we hold such beliefs, our world will naturally mirror them. But suppose that we believed that life's possibilities are limit-less, and that our path towards success and abundance lay in doing what we really love? Suppose that we abandoned all thoughts of what we 'should' do, or what feels safe and predictable, and followed the 'path with a heart'?

If we are willing to take a risk in order to follow our passion and enthusiasm, then everything else will fall into place. We will find ourselves in the right place at the right time. The means of making money will come quite readily

— and it will all be so enjoyable that it seems effortless.

Or perhaps you are already engaged in your life's work, but are unaware of its higher purpose? A friend who is a piano teacher used to wonder whether his work made a real contribution towards society, or whether there was something more 'important' that he should be doing. However, when he looked for the spiritual purpose behind his work, he found that it gave him the opportunity to be loving and positive, to pursue excellence, to bring joy to people, and to empower his pupils by helping them create music for themselves. He realised that he was not simply teaching the piano; that was just the vehicle through which he was pursuing his life focuses.

Whatever your life's work, it will feel natural and right. It will feel like coming home. Our work — whether paid, unpaid or voluntary — will enable us to radiantly express our inner self. All we need to become is who we are.

> *No apple tree tries to grow violets.*
>
> *(Seth)*[5]

YOUR LIFE'S WORK

1) If you have yet to discover your life's work, examine all the jobs you have had — including unpaid, voluntary and vacation work — and consider what knowledge and skills you gained from each. Each job will have been preparing you in some way for your life's work. Now make lists of your strengths, abilities and interests, what you enjoy doing, what you want from work and the global vision of the future which most inspires you.

Taken together, what sort of work might this lead towards? Which possibility most excites you? (If it doesn't excite you, it is not your life's work.) If necessary, silently ask your unseen friends for help in searching for your life's purpose.

2) Relax deeply, then imagine you are sitting on a riverbank. Use all your senses to make the scene come alive, to find yourself there in this peaceful scene. Now remove your footwear, and step into the river. Wade deeper and deeper, until you feel your feet being lifted by the current — and now allow yourself to be carried by the river's flow, floating along on the surface of the water. Watch the trees as you pass, as you follow the winding course of the river.

When you are ready, dive deep down into the river. Deeper and deeper, until the water becomes very still and quiet. Over to one side, you see a light — and you swim towards the light. It leads into an underground cavern, and before long you find yourself at the surface of the water, deep within the cavern. You swim to the sandy shore, and fall asleep.

You are woken by soft sounds behind you — footsteps upon the sand. You look around, and see an old man or old woman coming towards you. You see the love in their face, as they gaze into your eyes. Greet the old man or woman, and ask for their help in discovering your life's work. You will be given two gifts, hidden inside a small treasure chest. The first gift is a symbol of your life's work — a clue to where your great passion lies. Allow yourself to open the box, and remove the gift. Understand its message. (If it is unclear, then ask the old person for help.)

Now dig into the chest again, and find your second
gift — which represents a quality which you need in
order to begin, or continue, your life's work. Perhaps
it is courage, or love, or humour, or self-confidence,
or commitment, or wisdom, or vision. Let it be
whatever it is. (Again, if you do not understand, then
speak with your helper.)

Now thank the old person, and say goodbye.
Wade into the water, and swim deep down, following the light which guides you, finding your way
back. Swim up to the surface of the river, seeing the
sky and the trees, hearing the birdsong. Allow
yourself to flow with the river for a while. Then
gently come back to the room.

*Know that you are always being shown the next
step; it is always something that comes to mind
as an obvious, simple and joyful thing to do.*

(Orin)[6]

CHANGES

Orin often speaks of 'the void' — a time of transition when
we have outgrown our current way of life, but are unsure
where to go next. A time when we might feel lost,
frightened, lonely and confused. A time when we need to
be alone, to embrace our doubt and uncertainty, to
patiently trust in the enfolding darkness. During a void, we
can move beyond our blockages, and towards our life
focuses.

A void often occurs around the time of divorce or
separation, when a job no longer feels satisfying, when
children go to school or leave home, or when we yearn to

make some dramatic change — and when we enter a void, the future will seem blank or uncertain. At such times, it is crucial to let go of the past — to release the job, house, possessions, self-image, relationships or emotional patterns which are holding us back, so that we create space for the new. Often, we need to shut one door firmly behind us *without* knowing where the next door might open — to take a leap of faith which shows that we trust in the process of life.

At such times, Ego will usually attempt to obstruct or mislead us. The Ego is afraid of change. It prefers routine, security, sameness. It likes the present to repeat the past. Whenever we contemplate a change in lifestyle, career or relationships, Ego whispers in our ears — 'Better the devil you know!' — and reminds us of past failures and humiliations, while it secretly quakes in its little boots. Ego is not concerned with your happiness or fulfilment; it simply wishes to cling to the past. 'This might be awful, but at least it's familiar!'

The trouble is, unless we *overcome* our blockages and limitations, we are faced with them again and again — in different guises, perhaps, but the same old stumbling blocks. Unless we *deal* with our martyr, or fear of success, or suppressed anger, or belief that 'love hurts', then — since we create our own reality — it will reappear in life year after year, until we eventually learn the lesson.

We must release and move beyond our limiting beliefs and attitudes, self-pity, self-importance, negative scripts, lack of self-love, fear, guilt, blame, projections, avoiding responsibility, refusing to think, wanting guarantees, suppressing emotions, clinging to the past — everything which causes our misery and stuckness, which separates us from our Higher Self. As we do so — as we learn and change

— we can make quantum leaps towards creative, loving and expansive possibilities: our life focuses, our life's work, our Dreams.

The mundane world view assures us that causes lead to effects, that the past creates the present. But metaphysics suggests that, on the contrary, the future creates the present. We usually choose the *effect* we want, and then hunt around for a *cause*. If we decide we would like a common cold, for example, in order to spend a day or two in bed, Lazaris suggests we will *then* look for a draught, or hang around people who are sneezing — or if we are lazy, we won't bother with a 'cause' at all, but will simply manifest the 'effect' of the cold. Then at the first sign of headache and shivering, we say 'Oh no! I'm getting a cold!' — and cheerfully tuck ourselves into bed.

As Lazaris repeatedly states, 'The future creates the present against the backdrop of the past.' If we are heading towards a future which merely recreates the past, then our present life will reflect that — it will be repetitive and inflexible. If we are dreaming of more expansive possibilities, if we are Dreaming of the future, then the opportunities and experiences we will need are pulled towards us — and since the future is never predetermined, we can change our minds at any time, and choose a different 'probable self' to move towards. Desiring and imagining that new future will begin to change our present lives.

MAKING CHANGES

1) If your life feels stuck, or you cannot decide changes to make, do *anything* you would not normal to shake up your perceptions and rattle your old

habits. (An immediate way of doing this is to settle down, right now, in another part of the room — perhaps on or under the table, or in a corner, or behind the door. Then look around at the room from this perspective, as if you had never seen it before.)

Change your routine for a while. Make every day fresh and new. Try anything different — go roller skating, eat Mexican food, play a penny whistle, go to the cinema alone, take a stroll at sunrise, join a camera club, read a science fiction novel, rearrange the furniture, listen to Wagner, write a poem ... whatever you feel a crazy impulse to do. It doesn't matter that you might never want to do it again. It is doing something *different* that counts, exploring new possibilities.

2) Do you give yourself excuses for not changing? 'I'm too busy.' 'He/she won't let me.' 'I'm waiting until the children are older/until I retire/until I'm married/until ... ' 'I haven't enough money.' 'It would be selfish to do what I want to do.' What are your excuses? Be honest with yourself. What do you need to let go of, in order to move on?

3) Do you encourage your friends, partner, relatives or children to grow and change? Or do you express surprise or disapproval when they are unpredictable? 'But you *always* drink coffee!' 'You used to love your job!' 'You liked carrots *last* week!' 'Is this another of your crackpot schemes?' If so, how might you support them in reaching for the future?

FIVE YEARS ON

Relax deeply, then imagine a day in your life, five years from now — as you would like it to be. (This is one of your countless 'probable futures.') Picture yourself clearly. Where are you living? Who is important in your life? What is your work? What are your leisure interests? How have you changed as a person? What contribution are you making to society? What is your global vision — how would you like the world to be different in five years' time? (Try out several future selves, if you wish, until you find one that feels wonderful.) Now, as your future self, look back over the various steps that led towards this future, over the past five years. What advice do you wish to give to your 'self' of five years ago?

Gently come back to the room — then write down your Dream; consider the advice of your future self, and decide what you can do *today* to move towards that Dream. What could you do in the next month? Or six months? (The goals should make you feel alive, hopeful and 'tingly'; they will help you to become more of who you are. If they make you feel oppressed, unhappy or frightened, they are not part of your Dream.)

BRIDGE OF LIGHT

(This is a powerful meditation — adapted from LaUna Huffines' wonderful book, *Bridge of Light* —for connecting with a soul quality you need, in order to make positive life changes.)

Relax deeply, then imagine you are in a beautiful meadow. Use all your senses to make this scene come alive. Then walk up the mountain behind you. At the top you find a temple — your temple of Light. Picture every detail of this magnificent temple. As you enter the temple, you are greeted by a being of Light — perhaps your Higher Self or guide. Allow them to lead you where they will.

Tell the being of Light what you wish to do — perhaps to connect with a quality such as love, trust, courage, joy, humour or wisdom. Listen for any comments that the being of Light might make.

Now begin to spin a bridge of light. See the quality (perhaps as a symbol or colour) in the distance. Then imagine that a golden strand of light is emerging from your heart, and is connecting with that quality. More and more strands of light emerge from your heart, until you have built a bridge of light to the quality.

Attach the bridge of light to the temple, and begin to walk across the bridge. (You might find that the quality meets you on the bridge.) Allow yourself to bathe in the quality, absorbing its energy, for as long as you wish. Then gently come back to the room.

(Repeat this meditation several times for maximum effect. If your meditation does not follow the pattern above, that is fine — trust that whatever happens is right *for you*.)

> You will *awaken from the dream, either now or*
> *later. Why not now?*
>
> *(Bartholomew)*[7]

The more you see every situation, event, feeling, thought
and decision as a self-created opportunity, the easier it is
to view life as a glorious adventure — a giant chequer board,
in which you are shifting every pawn, every knight, every
bishop, castle, king and queen. Other people can and do
join in your game, and make a few moves here and there,
but they cannot shift a piece on your chequer board unless
you at least give your consent. After all, it's your game.

Letting go of the Realness of our lives is the doorway
to liberation. As we understand that our financial worries,
illness, marital conflicts, hassles at work, fears and
disappointments are all illusions that *we* have created in
order to learn and grow, in order to become who we are,
then we can look for the 'whisper' behind each experience,
and take appropriate action. Instead of getting stuck in
blame or self-pity, we can see that every challenge, whether
personal or global, is an opportunity — a chance to move
across our chequer board. As Bartholomew puts it, '
anything that comes to you is your friend'.[8]

Being a winner or loser is meaningless. It is how we play
the game that counts. Writing a best-selling novel, building
a business empire, founding a charity or being a famous
movie star is irrelevant; in the wink of an eye, all that will
be forgotten. It is *how* and *why* we create success in our
lives, what we *learn* from it, how much we *enjoy* it, how
much we *love* ourselves and others, whether we *grow*
spiritually that is significant. It is always the means, rather
than the end, that we need to focus upon. The goal is just
an illusion — merely a way of guiding our journey. It's the

moment-by-moment process, not the goal, that matters. Our journey is our destination.

As we awaken to our life focuses, our higher purpose, we awaken to our Dreams — not only our personal vision of what we might become, but our global vision of what the world might become. Although we create our own personal reality, we can affect the world. A principle we have created, within the illusion of physical reality, is that we either actively create *or passively allow* each and every event.

The joy of this lies in our potential to have impact upon the world. Not only can we create success in our own personal lives, but we can contribute towards *global* Dreams of the future. We *can* help others. We *can* love people. We *can* cherish our planet — *and make a difference.* Through our love, our hope, our joy, our vision, we can help to create a better world: the world of our Dreams.

9

Dance with the Angels

We shall not cease from exploration
And the end of all our exploring
Will be to arrive where we started
And know the place for the first time.

(T S. Eliot)[1]

In the myth of Psyche and Eros, the two lovers are separated while the goddess Aphrodite presents Psyche with four formidable tasks. First of all, Psyche is confronted with a roomful of mixed seeds and grains, and has to sort each variety into its own pile before nightfall. Fortunately, a colony of ants comes to her rescue, carrying each seed to its rightful place within the appointed time. In the second task, Psyche has to acquire some golden fleece from the aggressive, horned rams of the sun. She dare not even approach the rams for fear of being butted to death — until she is advised by a whispering reed to wait until sundown when the rams fall asleep, so that she can collect strands of golden fleece from the brambles. Psyche's third task is to fill a crystal flask from the River Styx, which flows from the highest summit down to the depths of the underworld, and up through the earth to emerge again at the heights. The stream runs through the steep mountains of Arcadia, and is guarded by dragons — but again help is at hand, in the form of an eagle, and the task is completed. For her final assignment, Psyche has to descend into the underworld, collect some ointment and return — ignoring the pleas of pathetic souls who will beg for her help. In despair, she climbs a high tower, resolving to leap to her death — but the tower advises her on how to complete her mission, and with the fourth task accomplished, an overjoyed Psyche is reunited with Eros.

The four tasks of Psyche might be compared with the spiritual journey towards Oneness. The first task — the sorting of grain — represents the need to continually sift through our beliefs, attitudes, thoughts and feelings, one by one, in order to become aware of the raw materials with which we create our reality. The second task — the golden fleece — symbolises the power of dominion rather than aggressive domination, as Psyche obviates the need to battle with the rams with the aid of the gentle, yielding reed. The third labour — the crystal flask — implores us to 'go with the flow', to trust our own intuition and impulses; while the eagle reminds us of the power of having personal Vision. The final task shows the necessity of descending into the underworld — with the help of transcendent wisdom, represented by the tower — to encounter and pass by the Ego.

All of Psyche's tasks were guided by the overwhelming power of love and culminate in Psyche's rediscovering her Oneness, no longer having to endure the pain of separation. Since time immemorial, spiritual teachers have informed us that we all stem from the same Source, that we are all divine sparks of *All That Is* — and that the illusion of separateness, and yearning for reunion, is the sole cause of pain. Our greatest driving force, say the mystics, is to search for our lost wholeness. (Religion literally means the re-connection (re-ligio) of humanity with the experience of Oneness.)

Channelled sources make it clear that the journey home does not mean losing our own uniqueness. We will never vanish into the great Oneness. Even our individual person-alities — being Chris or Emma or Joe — will never be lost. After all, time is just an illusion; therefore who we are now, who we have been and who we ever will be, is eternal. Spiritual growth means expanding *beyond* who we are 'now', becoming more of who we can be, not less. It is not by extinguishing our own light, or hiding it under a bushel, that we set off on our journey Home, but by *being* and *becoming* who we are, by developing as an individual, by expressing our unique Sparkness.

> *You become one with yourself through your*
> *love of yourself and all of the parts of you.*
> *There is no other way home, because you are*
> *home, and the wholeness of you is waiting.*
>
> *(Bartholomew)*[2]

ONENESS

Next time you are in a crowded place — perhaps a supermarket queue, busy shopping street, railway station or cafe — spend a few minutes looking around at the faces around you, seeing everyone here as part of you. Gaze at each person, accepting them totally as an aspect of yourself. See the God, the Light within each of them. Surround each person in white light, sending them your love. Allow yourself to merge with them all, experiencing your Oneness.

Listen out for any 'better than' or 'less than' judgements that might pass through your mind, and remind yourself that in judging others, we judge ourselves.

(This exercise can be a truly remarkable experience.)

Seek not outside yourself. For it will fail,
and you will weep each time an idol falls.
(A Course In Miracles)[3]

So — how do we get 'there' from 'here'? How do we find our way Home? Countless teachers, systems and techniques are strewn across our path, and our task is to resist the temptation to swallow undigested chunks of dogma — whether of metaphysics, Christianity, Buddhism, humanistic therapies or any other system of thought. While learning from others, we must guide our own journey Home. Rather than having blind faith in ancient or modern texts, gurus, therapists, or channelled sources, or seeking others' approval by adopting (or rejecting) fashionable beliefs, we need to doubt, question, think, feel and 'know' for ourselves. We need to be sceptical and discerning, to discover our *own* truth — recognising that this is *our* truth, rather than *the* Truth. 'There is no path in the sky,' warns the Dhammapada, 'and a monk must find the inner path.'[4]

In recent years, we have seen many 'false gurus', who have gathered a large following before being revealed as crazy or corrupt. The message is clear. We must no longer give away our power to outside authorities, to gurus, to dogma. Instead, we must listen to our own hearts, our inner guru. We must trust in our inner wisdom.

The journey Home is an *inner* journey — a path of self-discovery, not one of piety, hypocrisy, dogma and ritual. It is surely the Adolescent, desperate for certainty, which is responsible for our worshipping and guru-hopping — whether we 'worship' spiritual guides, therapeutic approaches, political systems, science and technology, or religion. And it is the Young Adult within who hardens our beliefs into rigid doctrine and fundamentalism. After all, the great spiritual teachers — including Jesus Christ and Buddha — have been heretics; they rejected the orthodoxy of their day, and sought the truth within their own hearts. We should all aim to be heretics, not out of rebellion, but through trusting our sense of inner knowing. The true spiritual journey, that of the Adult, is unique and intensely personal.

Spiritual growth is not measured by how many texts we read, words of wisdom we can quote, or meetings and workshops we attend; nor by how often we pray, meditate, process or programme. It is not an eager, frantic and undignified scramble to get 'there'! It is a question of whether we *live*, whether we *embody*, our wisdom in the here-and-now — indeed, whether it has become 'our' wisdom at all. Reading a few profound words with care, pondering their implications, breathing in their meaning, allowing them to transform our way-of-seeing the world, our way of being-in-the-world, is worth a hundred books which are rapidly skimmed and then returned to the library shelf.

Being interested in spiritual growth, but not yet involved in our own inner journey, is like being a wine connoisseur who might have scoured every book about fine wine, listened avidly to other experts, and who can recite every characteristic of named wines, but has never actually *tasted* wine. Our knowledge will be shallow, restricted and meaningless.

Teachers and techniques are merely signposts along our path — often useful, sometimes misleading, always temporary. As the Buddha said, a raft might be a good method of crossing the river, but on reaching the far shore, we should abandon the raft, not drag it across the land. (Alan Watts amusingly suggests that chronic Buddhism is even more common than chronic psychotherapy![5]) The techniques of metaphysics — processing, programming, meditations — are fingers pointing at the moon, not the moon itself.

> *The great path has no gate,*
> *Thousands of roads enter it.*
> *When one passes through this gateless gate*
> *He walks freely between heaven and earth.*
> (*Mumon*)[6]

Although we must forge our own way, our journey Home is crowded with unseen friends — and when the pupil is ready, the teacher appears. When we are ready to move on, the means will rapidly appear — a book or poster which catches our eye, a chance remark from a friend, a new acquaintance, an impulse or intuition, a revealing meditation, or perhaps a life-changing event. Our Higher Self is constantly alert to the merest hint of a desire to learn and grow, and will enthusiastically dangle opportunities in our path. We can then choose a detour to avoid these messages, stumble over them cursing and swearing, or welcome them as treasured and valuable gifts.

The myth of Psyche and Eros reminds us that help is always at hand — and channelled sources assure us that *every* call for help is heard. We need only ask, then remain alert for a reply. 'Ask!' says Orin. 'We cannot give you anything unless you ask. The universe waits for you to ask.'[7] Whatever the problem, if we silently ask for help, then wait expectantly, the help *will* come. Perhaps not in the form we expect, but it will come.

However, beseeching someone 'up there' to take pity on us, while sitting back in our armchair, will not do the trick. Our unseen friends will not rustle up a miracle while we twiddle our thumbs. Having a traditional fairy godmother would not aid our growth: 'I want a happy marriage', 'I desire a peaceful world', 'I wish to be a millionaire', and whoosh! our three wishes are granted, would teach us nothing. The point is to learn *how* to create loving relationships, *how* to create peace, *how* to create abundance — so that we can wave our own magic wands.

If you give someone a fish, you feed them for a day; but if you teach them how to fish, you feed them for a lifetime. Our unseen friends will, if requested, boost our own efforts, offer inspiration, or guide us towards the people or information that we need. But they will never cheat us of an opportunity to 'learn how to fish'. They will co-create *with* us, but will never do the work *for* us.

Whenever they *do* grace us with their friendly hints, comments and suggestions, whether directly or indirectly, it is wise to thank them. Gratitude — a wave of joy, with a feeling of thankfulness — is a gift, a powerful force, and an essential aspect of our spiritual growth. The more we appreciate ourselves, friends, family, colleagues, work, acquaintances, pets, society, the natural world, and the more we feel thankful for pleasures that we enjoy, successes that we create, and good news that we hear, the more we invite those joys to increase. The more we feel grateful towards our unseen friends, embracing the awareness of forces beyond ourselves, beyond physical reality, the more we expand our sense of who we are, and encourage further help and guidance.

Our unseen friends are many and varied: guides, counsellors, helpers, archetypes, guardian angels, channelled sources, our future self, Higher Self, the Christ consciousness and (ultimately) All That Is. Whether or not these beings are all 'real', in the sense that they exist beyond our own unconscious mind, is probably irrelevant, so long as they are caring and benevolent. (If an 'unseen friend' informs you that your mission is to save the world — *or* that you are the scum of the Earth — you can be quite sure that is your Ego speaking! The Ego enjoys disguising itself as a visitor from other realms, but if you know your Ego's tricks, you can usually spot it.)

Lazaris suggests[8] that each of us has two guides or counsellors — one male, one female — who might be figments of our imagination, aspects of our higher consciousness, or conscious beings in their own right; and that it matters not in the slightest which category our guides belong to. Imaginary guides can be just as helpful as any others. Again, it is Ego which longs for them to be Real!

My own guides — a slightly-built Indian woman named Amürtha, and a white-robed man, Saul, who glows with light — guide me in the use of metaphysical techniques. I often discuss my future plans and wishes with them, programme with them, or simply enjoy their company during meditations. Guides — whether 'real' or not — are wise, loving and respectful friends, and building a relationship with them is highly recommended.

MEETING YOUR GUIDES

Relax deeply, and imagine that you are standing at the bottom of a grassy hill. It is a bright, moonlit night. You hear owls hooting, trees rustling in the breeze, and a scurry of wildlife in the undergrowth. The air is sweetly scented.

Look up the hill, and see a circle of standing stones on the summit, haunting and mysterious in the moonlight. You climb up the gentle slope, and pass through two of the tall, flat stones into the circle. You see two shadows flit across the circle, as though two figures have hidden behind the stones at your approach, biding their time. You stand and wait, feeling safe, calm and expectant. A warm breeze flurries through the stones.

Before long, a woman and a man enter the circle from behind you, and slowly approach you. You feel their love envelop you. Allow yourself to see these two figures. What footwear does each have on? What clothes are they wearing? How tall are they? What are their facial features? What are your impressions of these two people?

Greet your guides, touching their hands or hugging them. Then ask their names. (You will probably 'hear' or 'see' the words, rather than hear your guides speaking directly.) Speak with your guides for as long as you wish, and thank them before you leave. Then gently come back to the room.

(If you find that only one guide appears — or several — that is fine. Trust your own experience.)

Although our guides — like our Higher Self — will assist in any aspect of our lives, we can engage more specific help if we wish. When we have a certain project, problem or situation to deal with, for example, we can request a helper for this particular task. As with our guides, we can meet and converse with this helper in meditation.

We can also reach out to our Future Self, perhaps to ask the probable outcome of decisions we might take. The Future Self is not just an abstract concept. After all, time is an illusion. Past, present and future are simultaneous. All of our probable futures are already happening. Our various probable Future Selves co-exist — and they are just as 'real' as we are. Just as we might be a Future Self to the five-year-old Child within us, our own Future Self offers us love, support and encouragement. Our Future Self knows what we have the potential to become. It can see where we are going. It can serve as our guide and mentor. It can help us to reach towards our Dreams.

> *Many people have at one time or another*
> *changed their present behaviour in response to*
> *the advice of a 'future' probable self, without ever*
> *knowing they have done so.*
>
> (Seth)[9]

YOUR FUTURE SELF

Imagine yourself wandering along a country lane, deep in snow. The scene is a winter wonderland, with crisp white snow blanketing the fields, hedge-rows and trees, glistening in the golden glow of the early morning sun. Snowflakes are still gently falling. Your footsteps crunch in the snow as you walk along, captivated by this dazzling landscape. Your breath turns to white in the cool air.

Suddenly you hear laughter behind you, and your Child appears — and tumbles into your waiting arms. Full of fun, it runs ahead and kicks at the snow in delight. Now you hear more footsteps approaching from behind — and your Adolescent is here. You hug warmly — and your Adolescent walks on, catching snowflakes in its hand, marvelling at their form. As you glance behind, you notice that your footsteps are disappearing under the fresh fall of snow.

The three of you stroll along the country lane, and you see a glowing light up ahead. As you move towards it, the light seems to move towards you. It is your Future Self. With your Child and Adolescent, you approach the glowing light. (Your Future Self might remain a light, or might take on a human form — looking, of course, like you.) Reach out and touch your Future Self, absorbing its energy and love.

(If you wish, repeat this meditation several times, and begin to communicate with your Future Self, just as you speak with your Child, Adolescent and guides. Remember that the future is never predetermined. Our Future Self can see the road ahead, because that is where it comes from; it can help us to choose our best possible future. But the choices are always ours.)

At turning points in life, or when we wish to leap to a new level of growth, we might wish to engage the archetypal energy which traditionally symbolises such transitions (and is sometimes said to materialise in physical reality): the old man or old woman. A client of mine, nearing the end of therapy, was leaving home to start a new life, studying for her chosen career. One day, while walking along the beach, Laura met an old man and, to her surprise, found herself confiding in this stranger. He was a gentle, kindly soul who listened intently. He warmly encouraged Laura in her vocation, and confessed of his great love for chrysanthemums. The encounter had a profound and empowering effect upon Laura. She later said, quite spontaneously: 'You remember that old man I told you about? I think he was an angel.'

Yet another set of unseen friends is the anima and animus—the 'feminine' and 'masculine' archetypes within each of us — represented by a woman and a man. At a soul level, of course, we are neither male nor female.

We have all experienced many lifetimes as women, and many lifetimes as men, learning different lessons from each. The soul does not have gender. But we have created a world in which 'feminine' and 'masculine' energy are polarised, so that we can reconcile the two. 'Feminine' energy is not confined to women, nor 'masculine' energy to men. They are two halves of the Self within us. Yet so often we squash one or the other side of our nature, or seek it in another person. At personal and global levels, our challenge is to reclaim our wholeness.

Patriarchal society, with its excess of 'masculine' power and energy, is responsible for many of the world's problems: the ruthless pursuit of power, the destructive exploitation of the natural world, the insanity of nuclear weapons, violence between nations, denigration of women, child abuse, racial oppression, lonely competitiveness and soul-less materialism. Patriarchy has created a raging monster, imprisoned by its own chains — and only the awakening Goddess can set it free.

The New Age vision is reliant upon the re-emergence of the 'feminine': cooperation, receptivity, sensitivity, imagination, emotionality, intuition, synthesis, conception, spiritual awareness. With the resurgence of the Goddess, we might learn once again how to live in harmony with each other, and with the planet.

We often assume that problem-solving requires an active, aggressive, scientific 'masculine' approach — but rational, logical, sequential thought is limited. Useful in its place, but limited. It lacks any inspiration, any creativity, any vision. 'Masculine' approaches to problem-solving will not help us conceive the future of our Dreams. It is not just a case of needing to *do* this and then that; we must *see* our challenges in a different way, shake up our old perceptions, trust our intuition, be prepared to take leaps of faith.

> *Through the harmony and ultimately the*
> *balance of that feminine energy, of that Goddess*
> *energy, you will unlock the Vortex of Power*
> *that lies within.*
>
>   *(Lazaris)*[10]

Feminine energy is not 'better than' masculine energy. Without masculine energy, the creative inspiration, hunches, desires, emotions, compassion, empathy and love which spring from the Goddess would never be *acted* upon. The feminine and the masculine are complementary forces in our reality, personally and globally.

However, the New Age invites us to celebrate the re-emergence of the Goddess: to learn to value feeling as much as thought, intuition as much as rationality, imagination as much as understanding, receptivity as much as assertiveness, synthesis as much as analysis, being as much as doing. Both women and men need to reclaim their feminine energy — not as a *replacement* for masculine energy, but as a crucial *balancing* force.

ANIMA AND ANIMUS

Relax deeply, then imagine you are on a deserted beach. Feel the warmth of the sun. Hear the waves crash against the shoreline. Taste the salty air. You feel at peace.

Now you sense a presence behind you, and a male figure appears at your right side. He is the masculine energy within you. Feel the strengths and positive qualities that he represents. You move closer together — and as you merge with him, you feel a marvellous surge of energy.

The sun is now setting on the horizon, casting a red glow across the water. The waves are lapping gently on the shore. Night falls — and you feel another presence nearby. At your left side, a female figure drifts into view, illuminated by the blue light of the full moon. Feel the energy and qualities that she represents. Now you move together, and merge into one another. You sense your body being filled with wondrous feminine energy, and you feel complete.

Watch now as the sun rises on another day. Enjoy your inner wholeness as you sit on the beach. Then gently come back to the room.

Sadly, 'spirituality' and 'God' have become rather dirty words in our materialistic age. Many of us close our hearts and minds at the very mention of such terms. The patriarchal religions of the Old Age still hang heavy upon us, conjuring up visions of the self-righteous martyr with a brave, weak smile; recital of sycophantic prayers to God-the-father; 'have mercy upon us for we are sinners'; fire and brimstone sermons; passive withdrawal and detachment from the world; the puritanical belief that suffering is good for the soul; or humble vows of poverty, chastity and obedience. According to Old Age thought, God commands us to be miserable, guilt-ridden, downtrodden ascetics who shun earthly pleasures, criticise and judge ourselves, and struggle through life in hope of a reward in heaven.

The New Spirituality implores us to reject this gobble-dygook. How could a loving God/dess be dictatorial, judgemental and punishing? If a wise, loving, creative Force exists — whatever we name that power — then that Force accepts us unconditionally as we are. It does not prefer some people to others, nor love us more if we are 'good'. It simply loves us, and wishes us to experience all of life's joy, success and abundance.

Of course, we should be wary of seeing the New Spirituality as 'better than' the old religions. Almost any spiritual belief holds the potential to transform our lives. Like any philosophy, metaphysics can easily be distorted and abused. We must each choose our own spiritual path — and learn to walk along that path in a loving, caring and empowering way.

As we learn how to joyously create our own reality — perhaps through processing, programming, releasing the past, letting go of our payoffs, accepting responsibility, loving self and others, working with unseen friends, awakening to our life purpose, and dreaming our Dreams — so we expand towards our Higher Self.

Our Higher Self is ever-present as a conscious energy field around us. It is what we are, what we are becoming, the butterfly emerging from our chrysalis. Our Higher Self knows the way Home. When we live through our Higher Self, when we resonate with its energy, we *are* Home, and as with other unseen friends, we can establish a loving relationship with our Higher Self and tune into its soft, reassuring voice.

One of my favourite meditations is simply to float in the midst of the vastness of my Higher Self, bathed in its love and light.[11] When I tried this for the first time, I was quite astounded at its impact. It was like being surrounded by a giant force field, electrified by its energy, whirring far beyond time and space, almost exploding with ecstasy. Afterwards, I burst into joyful tears of gratitude. I had initially approached the Higher Self as a pleasant idea for a meditation — but this memorable experience convinced me that something was Really happening, that the Higher Self was not just a theoretical notion, but a metaphysical reality. Soon after that, I met my personified Higher Self — and it felt like a blissful reunion, a sparkling celebration, a dazzling dance of delight.

As we awaken to our Higher Self, the magic and wonder of life becomes integral to our moment-by-moment aware-ness. Our everyday reality comes to include:

- inner peace and harmony
- spontaneous humour and delight
- waves of joy
- a deep sense of gratitude
- feeling complete in oneself
- being unhurried, and free from 'busyness'
- freedom from fear and struggle
- a sense of wonder and curiosity
- unlimited thinking
- energy and enthusiasm
- taking 'leaps of faith'
- speaking from the heart

- having the strength to be vulnerable
- self-respect and calm dignity
- expressing feelings and opinions openly
- trust in one's inner knowing
- willingness to trust others
- happiness in simply 'being'
- taking oneself lightly
- 'going with the flow'
- feeling fulfilled
- a sense of purpose and destiny
- creative inspiration
- focusing on the process rather than the goal
- having the courage to make commitments
- leading a balanced life
- seeing the larger picture
- taking 100 per cent responsibility for one's life
- feeling powerful
- giving from a sense of abundance
- compassion and respect for all beings
- reverence for the planet
- a sense of connectedness
- loving and forgiving oneself
- loving and forgiving others
- being honest
- being intimate
- having a positive impact upon the world
- forever changing and growing
- living in the present moment
- realising one's Dreams
- feeling 100 per cent alive.

BECOMING YOUR HIGHER SELF

Look through the checklist above, and consider how often you express or experience each of these qualities. Pick out three qualities which you particularly aspire to. Write out reminders to yourself on three small cards: Gratitude. Honesty. Compassion. Self-expression. Inner peace. Forgiveness. Process, not goal. Enthusiasm. And so on.

How might you act 'as if' you possessed these qualities? Make a list of how someone would think, feel and behave if they, say, felt intense gratitude, or were deeply compassionate, or accepted total responsibility for their lives? From now on, whenever you remember, try to act 'as if' you were this person, to invite your Higher Self into your everyday life.

Begin to think of yourself as (say) a grateful, compassionate and responsible person. How does it feel? Do you notice other changes in yourself, as you focus upon expressing these qualities?

MEETING YOUR HIGHER SELF

First of all, create a peaceful sanctuary in which to meet your Higher Self — perhaps a sunny meadow, a cave, a deserted beach or a grassy riverbank. Visit this sanctuary several times in meditation, preparing to meet your Higher Self. Sooner or later, you will feel another presence in your sanctuary — and know that your Higher Self has arrived. Allow it to bathe you in its love and light. Become one with your Higher Self.

Next time you visit the sanctuary, request that your Higher Self appears in human form. Allow yourself to see, to touch, to experience, to love and be loved by your personified Higher Self. Ask for its name. Begin to build up a trusting and intimate relationship with this long-lost friend.

In time, you might find that your Higher Self enters many of your meditations, offering loving guidance and support — and that, more and more, you 'hear' its voice while in a waking state. You are becoming one with your Higher Self.

You are a vast, brilliant, extending, creative energy field that exploded out of the Heart of the One and is delighting in its journey Home.
> (Bartholomew)[12]

Becoming aware that we create our own reality is not an all-or-nothing realisation. Even when it comes as a breathtaking moment of insight, a flash of 'cosmic con-sciousness', we keep slipping back into our old beliefs and payoffs. We fall into periods of doubt and fear, wondering whether we are being naive and gullible, whether we are kidding ourselves. We cling to 'pockets of Realness' in our lives — perhaps accepting that we can create success at work or good health, but seeing money or relationships as quite beyond our control. Or we might believe that we create our own *personal* reality, but cannot have an impact on the outside world. All of this confusion is part of our journey, part of learning and growing. Gradually, we come to embody our new awareness, moment by moment, enraptured and enchanted by this thrilling adventure of being alive.

If we wish to dance with the angels, it is not necessary to sprout wings or sign on for harp lessons. We simply need to become ourselves — to express our uniqueness, realise our own potential, consciously create our own reality — and have fun doing so. We should not try to be perfect, but rather to be perfectly ourselves.

Lazaris frequently reminds us that the steps to getting there are the same as the qualities of being there. The process is the goal. The means is also the end. For the paradox is that we are already Home — the prize is already won. The problem is that we refuse to unwrap our prize, suspecting the gift-wrapped and garlanded box to be empty or booby-trapped, believing there must be a catch somewhere, that it cannot be so easy. But channelled sources assure us that we created Earth as our playground, a place in which to joyfully explore our limitless potential. Life was never meant to be full of pain and suffering. As the New Age approaches, it is time for us to wake up. It is time to learn how to have fun. It is time to create a world full of love, light and joy.

HEALING THE PLANET

Think of a global problem which concerns you, which touches your heart — perhaps a famine-stricken area, a war zone, factory farming, homelessness in your own city, political prisoners or nuclear stockpiles.

Devote 10-15 minutes, on a regular basis, to sending healing light and energy to this problem on the inner planes — perhaps focusing on those who need to take positive action, or make new choices (regardless of whether you know who they are).

Relax deeply, then mentally send whatever soul quality is most needed — perhaps love, peace, trust, wisdom, compassion or courage. Allow this quality to take the form of a coloured light — whatever colour feels right — and bathe the people or area in that colour. Know that this healing energy *will* have an impact. Then gently come back to the room.

Spirituality is often said to be airy-fairy and philosophical — all very well for Sunday mornings, but not very relevant to such practical problems as the disappearing rainforests, nuclear waste and terrorism. But this assumes that the world is Real — that we are spiritual beings only after we die (if at all), and that metaphysics is just an entertaining parlour game. But we do create our own reality — every single aspect of it. The world is an illusion that *we* create, and metaphysics is just as relevant to world politics and ecological threats as it is to our personal lives.

By having Dreams of a future in which the balance of nature is restored, radioactive waste has been rendered hazard-free, and people live in peace and harmony, we begin to create that reality, to make new choices, to Dream of new solutions which now seem impossible, solutions which lie beyond the looking glass. By believing it to be possible, it might become probable. By believing it to be probable, we might make it happen.

Through the power of thought, the power of consciousness, the power of love, who knows what we might be
capable of? Transmuting the greenhouse gases? Turning
barren deserts into lush green fields? Rendering nuclear
weapons harmless? Let us not limit ourselves to what the
mundane world view says is possible, or what the cynics
would have us believe. Let us be visionaries. Let us have
faith in the twenty-first century — not by burying our heads
in the sand, but by refusing to support the prophets of
doom-and-gloom, by knowing that we have created our
global problems for a reason, and there *will be* solutions.

Let us Dream of a New Age — an age of love, peace,
harmony, cooperation and spiritual awareness — and *know*
that it will be so. And let us — each of us — actively and joyfully
participate, in our own unique way, in making those
Dreams come true. Let us begin to live magically. Let us
begin to live our Dreams.

> *Come to the edge, he said,*
> *They said: We are afraid.*
> *Come to the edge, he said.*
> *They came.*
> *He pushed them ...*
> *... and they flew.*[13]

Footnotes

Frontispiece: A Course In Miracles, Vol 1, 365

PART ONE

1: A trick of the light? [1]Schumacher (1978) 155 [2] Mair (1989) 171 [3] Quoted in Ferguson (1982) 125 [4] Ferguson (1982) 30 [5] Russell (1988) vii [6] Lao Tzu (1963) 108 [7] Capra (1976) [8] Zukav (1980) [9] Bohm (1980) [10] Davies (1984) [11] Zukav (1980) 212 [12] eg quoted in Talbot (1981) 16 [13] eg see Sheldrake (1987), Prigogine and Stengers (1984), Watson (1980) [14] eg see Targ and Puthoff (1978) [15] Interview with Elisabeth Kubler-Ross, 'Kindred Spirit', 1989, Vol 1, No 9, 13-14 [16] Quoted in Ferguson (1982) 215 [17] Cornford (1941), 222-6 [18] Quoted in Klimo (1988) 13 [19] From 'Auguries Of Innocence', Blake (1982) 132 [20] Davies (1982) 13 [21] Quoted in Ferguson (1982) 187 [22] Quoted in Talbot (1988) 180 [23] Talbot (1988) 182 [24] Quoted in Toben and Wolf (1983) 126 [25] Robert Jastrow, quoted in MacLaine (1984) 356 [26] Stryk and Ikemoto (1981) 46 [27] see Bohm (1980) [28] James (1977) 374 [29] Quoted in Huxley (1985) 181 [30] Roberts (1987a) 10 [31] Roberts (1987a) 65 [32] Bartholomew (1987) ii [33] Roman (1986a) 5-6 [34] Lazaris (1988a) 26-7 [35] Klimo (1988) 5 [36] If you wish to learn how to channel, I strongly recommend Roman and Packer (1987) [37] Rodegast (1987) 5.

2: Beyond the bridge of belief [1] 'A Course In Miracles', Vol I, 553 [2] Capra (1983) 323 [3] Roberts (1974) 46 [4] White Eagle (1967) 16 [5] Lazaris, 'Reality Creation: The Basics' [6] Carey (1982) 42 [7] Roberts (1987b) 402 [8] Lazaris, 'Harnessing

The Power Of Your Destiny' [9] Roberts (1987b) *403* [10] Roberts (1974) *10* [11] Roberts (1987a) *211* [12] eg *see* Harrison and Harrison (1983), Iverson (1977), Wambach (1979); the latter includes unusual statistical evidence of reincarnation.[13] From 'Intimations of Mortality from Recollections of Early Childhood' (Hayward, 1956) *264* [14] Roberts (1987a) *146* [15] From 'Sudden Light' (Hayward, 1956) *363* [16] Roberts (1987a) *235* [17] Rodegast (1989) *62* [18] 'A Course In Miracles', Vol 1, 7 [19] Bartholomew (1986) *36* and *68* [20] Roberts (1987b) *480* [21] Bartholomew (1986) *13* [22] Quoted in Russell (1988) *40* [23] Bartholomew (1986) *56* [24] Lazaris (1988b) *116* [25] Roberts (1987a) *238* [26] Lazaris (1988a) *88* [27] eg *see* Talbot (1988) Chapter 7 [28] Davies (1984) *189* [29] Sheldrake (1987) *209-10* [30] Capra (1983) *67* [31] Quoted in Huxley (1985) *251* [32] Carey (1982) *52* [33] Bartholomew (1986) *148* [34] Quoted in frontispiece of Davies (1984) [35] Bartholomew (1989) *26* [36] 'A Course In Miracles,' Vol 1, *42* [37] Roberts (1974) *341* [38] Roberts (1974) *462* [39] Lazaris (1988b) *139* [40] *see* Roberts (1974) *370-3* [41] Stryk and Ikemoto (1981) *76*.

PART TWO
1: The Inner Journey [1] Roberts (1987b) 152 [2] Ferrucci (1982) 143 [3] Mair (1989) 141 [4] Roberts (1987c) 96 [5] Roads (1990) 74 [6] Bartholomew (1989) 22.

2: Take One Cosmic Egg [1] Roberts (1974) 436 [2] Roman (1986b) 96 [3] Bartholomew (1987) 26 [4] Bartholomew (1987) 153 [5] 'Eternity', Blake (1982) 46 [6] Roberts (1974) 36.

3: Through the Looking Glass [1] Carroll (1962) From 'Through The Looking Glass', 347 [2] Roberts (1987b) 53 [3] 'A Course In Miracles,' Vol 1, 418 [4] Widely quoted eg Trine (1989) 194 [5] Bartholomew (1986) 14 [6] Quoted in Klimo

(1988) 13 [7] Roberts (1974) 75 [8] Lazaris (1988a) 197 [9] White and Swainson (1971) 103 [10] For Lazaris programming techniques, *see* for example: 'Secrets of Manifesting What You Want', 'Programming What You Want', 'New Dynamics Of Processing And Programming' [11] Lazaris, 'The Mystery and Magic of Co-Creation' [12] Herrigel (1985) 46 [13] Lazaris (1987) xiii.

4: Cracks in the Mirror [1] Quoted in Wilber (1980) [2] 'A Course In Miracles', Vol I, 57 [3] Lazaris, 'Busting And Building Ego' [4] Lazaris, 'The Crisis Of Martyrhood' [5] Lazaris, [5] 'The Crisis Of Martyrhood' [6] eg Lazaris, 'Reality Creation: The Basics [7] Bartholomew (1989) 37 [8] From 'The Wasteland', Eliot (1954) 65 [9] See Boyle J, 'A Sense of Freedom' (Pan, 1977) and 'The Pain of Confinement' (Pan, 1985) [10] 'The Dhammapada' (1973) 81 [11] Bartholomew (1987) 46.

5: Listening to the Whispers [1] Reps (1971) 111 [2] Rodegast (1989) 26 [3] 'A Course In Miracles', Vol 1, 151 [4] Bartholomew (1989) 24 [5] 'A Course In Miracles', Vol 1, 78 [6] Roberts (1974) 475 [7] Roman (1986b) 130-1 [8] Roberts (1982) 246 [9] eg *see* Bandler and Grinder (1979) [10] 'A Course In Miracles', Vol II, 187.

6: What is Really Real? [1] Quoted in Huxley (1985) 323 [2] Williams (1986) [3] Roberts (1987a) 166 [4] Lazaris, 'Activating Miraculous Success' [5] Bartholomew (1986) 18 [6] Keyes (1974) 27 [7] Lazaris 'Healing And Releasing Hurt' [8] Howard (1967) 254 [9] 'A Course In Miracles', Vol 1, 77 [10] Bartholomew (1987) 57 [11] Rodegast (1987) 111 [12] Lazaris, 'Fear: The Internal War' [13] Mair (1989) 128 [14] Bartholomew (1989) 12 [15] Roman (1989) 79 [16] Roberts (1987a) 16 [17] Hay (1988) [18] Bartholomew (1986) 64.

7: Into the Shadowlands [1] From 'Fern Hill' (Hayward, 1956) 461 [2] Lazaris, 'Discovering The Adult' [3] Spitz R A, Anaclitic depression, 'Psychoanalytic Study Of The Child', 1946, Vol 2 313-342 [4] 'A Course In Miracles,' Vol II, 210 [5] Roman (1986a) 34 [6] Lao Tzu (1983) 129 [7] Lazaris, 'The Young Adult' [8] Berne (1962) 158 [9] A Course In Miracles', Vol 1 229 and 233 [10] eg Roberts (1987a) 218, Roberts (1974) 102 [11] Roman (1989) 123 [12] Lazaris, 'Your Future Self' (Seth similarly speaks of future neuronal structures: eg Roberts (1987b) 332 and 493).

8: Awakening to Your Dream [1] 'As You Like It', Act 2, Scene 7 140-143 [2] Lazaris, 'Harnessing The Power Of Your Destiny' [3] Mair (1989) 103 [4] Roman and Packer (1988) 67 [5] Roberts (1987b) 35 [6] Roman (1986a) 22 [7] Bartholomew (1989) 8 [8] Bartholomew (1987) 180.

9: Dance with the Angels [1] From 'Little Gidding' (Hayward, 1956) 442 [2] Bartholomew (1986) 43 [3] 'A Course In Miracles', Vol 1, 573 [4] 'The Dhammapada' (1973) 72 [5] Watts (1971) 83 [6] Roman (1989) 97 [7] Reps (1971) 94 [8] Lazaris, 'The Unseen Friends' [9] Roberts (1987b) 495 [10] Lazaris (1988a) 98 [11] For an enchanting series of Higher Self meditations, see Lazaris (1987) [12] Bartholomew (1987) 193 [13] Guillaume Apollinaire, quoted eg in Ferguson (1982) 322.

Bibliography

Ashley N, *Create Your Own Reality: A Seth Workbook*, Prentice Hall Press, New York, 1987.

Bach R, *Jonathan Livingston Seagull*, Pan, London, 1973.

Bandler B and Grinder J, *Frogs Into Princes*, Real People Press, Moab, Utah, 1979.

Bartholomew, *I Come As A Brother*, High Mesa Press, Taos, New Mexico, 1986.

Bartholomew, *From The Heart Of A Gentle Brother*, High Mesa Press, Taos, New Mexico, 1987.

Bartholomew, *Reflections Of An Elder Brother*, High Mesa Press, Taos, New Mexico, 1989.

Bentov I, *Stalking The Wild Pendulum*, Destiny Books, Rochester, Vermont, 1988. (First published 1977.)

Berne E, *Games People Play*, Penguin, Harmondsworth, 1968.

The Bhagavad Gita, Penguin, Harmondsworth, 1962.

Blake W, *Selected Poems* (ed. P H Butter), Dent, London, 1982.

Bohm D, *Wholeness And The Implicate Order*, Routledge and Kegan Paul, London, 1980.

Briggs J P and Peat F D, *Looking Glass Universe*, Fontana, London, 1985.

Capra F, *The Tao Of Physics*, Fontana, London, 1976.

Capra F, *The Turning Point*, Fontana, London, 1983.

Carroll L, *Alice's Adventures In Wonderland and Through The Looking Glass*, Penguin, Harmondsworth, 1962. (First published 1865 and 1872.)

Carey K, *The Starseed Transmissions,* Uni*Sun, Kansas City, MO, 1982.

Castaneda C, *The Teachings Of Don Juan,* Penguin, Harmondsworth, 1970.

Cornford F M (transl.), *The Republic of Plato,* Oxford University Press, London, 1941.

A Course In Miracles, Arkana, London, 1985. (First published 1975.)

Davies P, *Other Worlds,* Sphere, London, 1982.

Davies P, *God And The New Physics,* Penguin, Harmondsworth, 1984.

Davies P, *The Cosmic Blueprint,* Unwin Hyman, London, 1989.

The Dhammapada, Penguin, Harmondsworth, 1973.

Einstein A, *The World As I See It,* Bodley Head, London, 1935.

Eliot T S, *Selected Poems,* Faber and Faber, London, 1954.

Emmanuel — see Rodegast P.

Ferguson M, *The Aquarian Conspiracy,* Paladin, New York, 1982.

Ferrucci P, *What We May Be,* Turnstone, Wellingborough, Northants, 1982.

Gawain S, *Creative Visualisation,* Bantam, New York, 1982.

Gawain S and King L, *Living In The Light,* Eden Grove, London, 1988.

Gooch S, *The Double Helix Of The Mind,* Wildwood House, London, 1980.

Happold, F C, *Mysticism,* Penguin, London, 1963.

Harrison P and M, *Life Before Birth,* Futura, 1983.

Hay L L, *You Can Heal Your Life,* Eden Grove, London, 1988.

Heisenberg W, *Physics And Beyond,* Allen and Unwin, London, 1971.

Herrigel E, *Zen In The Art Of Archery*, Arkana, London, 1985. (First published 1953.)

Hoff B, *The Tao of Pooh*, Methuen, London, 1982.

Howard V, *The Mystic Path to Cosmic Power*, Parker, West Nyack, NY, 1967.

Huffines L, *Bridge Of Light*, Bantam, London, 1990.

Huxley A, *The Perennial Philosophy*, Triad Grafton, London, 1985. (First published 1946.)

Inglis B, *The Paranormal: An Encyclopaedia Of Psychic Phenomena*, Paladin, 1986.

Iverson J, *More Lives Than One?*, Pan, London, 1971.

James W, *The Varieties Of Religious Experience*, Fount/ Collins, London, 1977. (First published 1902.)

Jeffers S, *Feel The Fear And Do It Anyway*, Century Hutchinson, London, 1987.

Jones R, *Physics As Metaphor*, Abacus, London, 1983.

Keyes K, *Handbook To Higher Consciousness*, Living Love Center, Berkeley, California, 1974.

Klimo J, *Channelling*, Aquarian, Wellingborough, Northants, 1988.

Kuhn T S, *The Structure Of Scientific Revolutions*, University Of Chicago, Chicago, 1962.

Lao Tzu, *Tao Te Ching*, Penguin, Harmondsworth, 1963.

Lao Tzu, *The Way Of Life (Tao Te Ching)*, New American Library, 1983.

Lazaris, *The Sacred Journey: You And Your Higher Self*, Concept: Synergy, Beverly Hills, CA, 1987.

Lazaris, *Lazaris Interviews Book I*, Concept: Synergy, Beverly Hills, CA, 1988a.

Lazaris, *Lazaris Interviews Book II*, Concept: Synergy, Beverly Hills, CA, 1988b.

MacLaine S, *Out On A Limb*, Bantam, New York, 1986.

Mair M, *Between Psychology and Psychotherapy: A Poetics*

Of Experience, Routledge, London and New York, 1989.

Marlow M E, *Handbook for The Emerging* Woman, Donning, Norfolk, Virginia, 1988.

Needleman J, *A Sense Of The Cosmos,* Dutton, New York, 1976.

Orin — see Roman S.

Prigogine I and Stengers I, *Order Out Of Chaos,* Bantam, New York, 1984.

Reps P, *Zen Flesh, Zen Bones,* Penguin, Harmondsworth, 1971.

Roads M, *Journey Into Nature,* H J Kramer, Tiburon, CA, 1990.

Roberts J, *Seth Speaks,* Bantam, New York, 1974.

Roberts J, *Adventures In Consciousness,* Bantam, New York, 1979.

Roberts J, *The Individual And The Nature Of Mass Events,* Prentice Hall, New Jersey, 1982.

Roberts J, *The 'Unknown' Reality, Vol. 1: A Seth Book,* Prentice Hall, New York, 1986a. (First published 1977.)

Roberts J, *The 'Unknown' Reality, Vol. 2: A Seth Book,* Prentice Hall, New York, 1986b. (First published 1979.)

Roberts J, *The Seth Material,* Prentice Hall, New York, 1987a. (First published 1970.)

Roberts J, *The Nature Of Personal Reality: A Seth Book,* Prentice Hall Press, New York, 1987b. (First published 1974.)

Roberts J, *The Nature Of The Psyche: A Seth Book,* Prentice Hall Press, 1987c. (First published 1979.)

Roberts J, *The God Of Jane,* Prentice Hall Press, 1987d. (First published 1981.)

Rodegast P, *Emmanuel's Book,* Bantam, New York, 1987.

Rodegast P, *Emmanuel's Book II,* Bantam, New York, 1989.

Roman S, *Living With Joy,* H J Kramer, Tiburon, CA, 1986.

Roman S, *Personal Power Through Awareness,* H J Kramer, Tiburon, CA, 1986.

Roman S and Packer D, *Opening To Channel,* H J Kramer, Tiburon, CA, 1987.

Roman S and Packer D, *Creating Money,* H J Kramer, Tiburon, CA, 1988.

Roman S, *Spiritual Growth: Being Your Higher Self,* H J Kramer, Tiburon, CA, 1989.

Russell P, *The Awakening Earth,* Arkana, London, 1988. (First published 1982.)

Schumacher E F, *A Guide For the Perplexed,* Abacus, London, 1978.

Seth — see Roberts J.

Sheldrake R, *A New Science Of Life,* Paladin, London, 1987. (First published 1981.)

Stryk L and Ikemoto T (transl.), *The Penguin Book Of Zen Poetry,* Penguin, Harmondsworth, 1981.

Talbot M, *Mysticism And The New Physics,* Bantam, New York, 1981.

Talbot M, *Beyond The Quantum,* Bantam, New York, 1988.

Targ R and Puthoff H, *Mind-Reach,* Paladin, London, 1978.

Teilhard de Chardin P, *The Phenomenon Of Man,* Collins, London and New York, 1959.

Tillich P, *The Courage To Be,* Collins, London, 1977. (First published 1952.)

Toben B and Wolf F A, *Space-Time and Beyond,* Bantam, New York, 1983.

Trine R W, *In Tune With The Infinite,* Unwin Hyman, London, 1989. (First published 1899.)

The Upanishads, New American Library, New York, 1957.

Wambach H, *Reliving Past Lives,* Hutchinson, London, 1979.

Watkins S M, *Conversations With Seth, Vol. 1,* Prentice Hall, New York, 1980.

Watkins S M, *Conversations With Seth, Vol. 2,* Prentice Hall, New York, 1986.

Watson L, *Lifetide,* Hodder and Stoughton, London, 1979.

Watts A, *Psychotherapy East And West,* Random House, New York, 1971.

White Eagle, *Wisdom From White Eagle,* White Eagle Publishing Trust, Liss, Hants., 1967.

White R and Swainson M, *Gildas Communicates,* C W Daniel, Saffron Waldon, Essex, 1971.

Wilber K, *The Atman Project,* Theosophical Publishing House, Wheaton, Ill., 1980.

Wilde S, *Affirmations,* White Dove International, Taos, NM, 1987.

Wilde S, *The Force,* White Dove International, Taos, NM, 1984.

Wilde S, *Miracles,* White Dove International, Taos, NM, 1983.

Williams M, *The Velveteen Rabbit,* Carousel, London, 1986.

Wolman B B (ed), *Handbook Of Parapsychology,* Van Nostrand Reinhold, New York, 1977.

Zukav G, *The Dancing Wu Li Masters,* Fontana, London, 1980.

Zukav G, *The Seat of The Soul,* Simon and Schuster, New York, 1989.

The following Lazaris audiotapes (Concept, Synergy, Beverley Hills/Florida) were also used:

Abundance: The Skill; Activating Miraculous Success; Balance: Releasing The Full Self; Busting And Building Ego; Busting And Building Image; Conceiving/Perceiving; Consciously Creating Success; The Crisis of Martyrhood; Developing A Relationship With Your Higher Self (video); Developing Self-Confidence; Discovering The Adult; Discovering Your Subconscious; The Elegance Of Abundance; Ending Guilt; Ending Self-Sabotage; Ending Shame; Fear: The Internal War; Freedom: Its Mystery And Power; Harnessing The Power Of Your Destiny; Healing: The Nature of Health, Parts I and II; I Deserve; Inner Peace; Intimacy and Loving Relationships; Intuition; Living Magically Every Day; Loving; The Mystery And Magic Of Co-Creation; The New Age And Its Future; New Dynamics Of Processing And Programming; On Releasing Hurt/The Keys of Happiness; Personal Power And Beyond; Positive Ambition; Programming What You Want; Reality Creation: The Basics; The Secrets Of Manifesting What You Want I and II; Stop Feeling Not Good Enough; Stumbling Blocks/Building Blocks; The Unseen Friends; Winning The Manifestation Game; The Young Adult; Your Emotional Strengths; Your Future Self; Your Uniqueness.

For further details of Lazaris workshops, books, CDs DVDs, downloads etc. See:
www.lazaris.com

Concept: Synergy
P.O. Box 3285
Palm Beach,
FL 33480.
U.S.A.

For further details of Orin workshops, books,
audio courses, CDs etc., See:

LuminEssence,
P.O. Box 1310,
Medford
OR 97501
U.S.A.

For further details about workshops with Gill Edwards on
reality creation and conscious medicine, plus books, CDs,
Lakeland Essences etc, please contact:

Living Magically
Fisherbeck Mill
Old Lake Road
Ambleside
Cumbria LA22 ODH
Tel: (015394) 31943
Fax: (015394)31946
E-mail: LivMagic@aol.com

CD titles currently include: Overcoming Inner Blockages,
Healing or Releasing Relationships, Healing Your Inner Child,
The Morning CD, Soul Retrieval, Attracting a Soulmate,
Creating Prosperity, Inner Peace, Changing Your Beliefs,
Wish Upon a Star (for children), Your Future Self and
Healing Disease.

Website: www.livingmagically.co.uk

Index

Capitalised entries denote exercises

Wild Love
Gill Edwards
978 0 7499 2687 8

Unconditional or 'wild' love sets us free to be who we are

In *Wild Love* clinical psychologist and metaphysical writer Gill Edwards reveals a deeper, more magical reality where you can break free from the 'ego prisons' of fear and guilt and start to love yourself, other people and life, unconditionally.

Gill explains that your ego can short-circuit your energies and make you always look for approval, safety and control in your relationships. She explains that when we learn to enjoy unconditional *wild* love, we will set ourselves free to follow our dreams.

- Learn to connect with a deeper reality and become an embodied soul – loving, joyful, creative, passionate and full of gratitude.
- Start to say 'yes' to life instead of 'no' or 'maybe' or 'only if'.
- Get your energy flowing again so you can connect with unconditional love and remember who you truly are.

This beautifully written and inspiring book will teach you how to change your life from the inside out, and discover your unique potential.